OLD-TIME
TELEVISION
MEMORIES

by Mel Simons

Also by Mel Simons:

The Old-Time Radio Trivia Book

The Old-Time Television Trivia Book

Old-Time Radio Memories

The Show-Biz Trivia Book

OLD-TIME TELEVISION MEMORIES

by Mel Simons

BearManor Media
2009

Old-Time Television Memories

For information, address:

BearManor Media
P. O. Box 71426
Albany, GA 31708

bearmanormedia.com

Cover design by John Teehan

Typesetting and layout by John Teehan

Published in the USA by BearManor Media

ISBN—1-59393-319-3

Dedication

This book is dedicated to my two grand neices,
Sarah and Willow Goldman

Mel Simons

Table of Contents

Foreword by Bill Dana i

A Word of Thanks iii

George Jessel 1

Milton Berle 7

Willard Waterman 13

Morey Amsterdam 27

Clayton Moore 35

Sheldon Leonard 43

Steve Allen 55

Perry Como 79

Gale Storm 87

Soupy Sales 107

Joe Franklin 113

Mickey Freeman 117

Larry Storch 125

Foreword
by Bill Dana

A huge "Thank You" should go to whatever Force gave the gift of reverence for things past to Mel Simons.

The invention of the computer and its potential for permanent archiving somewhat diminishes the threat of loss of past glory but a computer, at least mine, just sits there and could care less what Jack Benny's real name is. Hence, it is appropriate to heartily acknowledge those individuals, such as the dedicated media historian Mel Simons, who create via their documentation and recordation, "Gifts Which Keep on Giving."

Thank you, Mel!

– Bill Dana

Many know Bill Dana as "José Jiménez," a popular character he created on *The Steve Allen Show* in the 1950s and continued to perform throughout the '60s. But Dana has also been a successful writer, author, cartoonist, producer, director, recording artist, inventor and stand-up comedian. For more information on this comic talent, please check out his web site at www.bill-dana.com.

A Word of Thanks...

I am very grateful to the people who made this book possible: the television performers who graced the small screen during its heyday.

It has been my pleasure not only to interview, but to introduce many of these personalities on various stages throughout the years.

– Mel Simons

George Jessel

George Jessel

GEORGE JESSEL (APRIL 3, 1898-MAY 23, 1981) could seemingly do it all: He was a comedian, an actor, a singer/songwriter, and an Academy Award-winning movie producer. In vaudeville he was known for his mock-telephone conversations with his mother ("Hello, Mama? It's your son Georgie, from the money every week."). On television he was a frequent guest on the talk shows hosted by Jack Paar, Mike Douglas, Merv Griffin and Johnny Carson. Jessel is perhaps best remembered as the "Toastmaster General of the United States," a title he was given in recognition of his many speeches at political and entertainment events. He was also a notorious "ladies' man." The first time I met him, he tried to steal my girlfriend. He was eighty years old at the time. (We laughed about it later.)

Georgie was always at home in front of a live audience, as he proved during our joint appearance at the Brickman Hotel in South Fallsburg, New York on April 14, 1979.

Mel   There are so many wonderful things that I could say about Mr. George Jessel. He has done and accomplished so much throughout the years. So I think to make it brief, I'll read a few notes taken from an editorial in *The New York Post* by Earl Wilson.

And I quote: "A man who is a legend in his own time. Actor, author, producer, songwriter. The most decorated civilian from the military in America, including the Purple Heart. Ladies and gentlemen—named by five presidents The Toastmaster General of the United States"—
It is my great honor and privilege to present...George Jessel.

(Applause)

G.J.   I particularly want to thank Mel for his very warm introduction, and while listening to it for a moment I thought I was dead!

1

(Laughter)

G.J.   This is a remarkable place, this Brickman Hotel. I came here many, many years ago, and it's remarkable to see how well it's been kept up. I had the same napkins at my table that I had 25 years ago.

(Laughter)

G.J.   I get a great kick coming here and seeing these many people, who have known me from my long career. Now, Mel, anything that you would like to ask me about my background, about my political life, about some of my romantic episodes, go right ahead. I want you to know as practically my biographer, Mel here, this guy knows more about me than my mother did, I think! I'm qualified to speak about the theatre, motion pictures, about television, and about good music, literature, and the letter of religion.

I've never been Bar Mitzvah. I've never had any religious education. I've never had any scholastic education but for eight months, between the ages of eight and nine.

At the age of nine I was the batboy for the New York Giants Baseball Club, under John McGraw. Since then I've been in the amusement business nearly all of my life. So Mel, any questions that you want to throw at me I'd be happy to answer.

Mel   George, I would like to begin by asking you about one of the most lovable gentlemen in show business. I know you were a great friend of this person, Eddie Cantor. Would you comment a little bit on your association with Eddie Cantor?

G.J.   Well, Eddie Cantor was the first showman or important actor that, after a show, instead of looking in the mirror and still hearing the applause of the audience in his ears, he'd look out the window of the dressing room that came out to a dirty alley. He would see if there was anybody there less fortunate than he so that he could be helpful to him.

He did more for the social scene than any other actor that ever lived. When he was very ill and when I saw he was near death, I went to Washington, D.C. I asked President John Kennedy to give him a citation for what he had done to help all people less fortunate. Mr. Kennedy said, "I'm going to do a lot of that in July. I'll put him down, and one for you, too"

I said, "Thank you." But he didn't do it. So I asked Lyndon Johnson, who was the Vice President. Two weeks after Lyndon Johnson became President of the United States he sent a citation to Governor Brown and to me, which we delivered to Eddie Cantor. That is what made me love Lyndon Johnson all these years.

Eddie was much older than I. When I was a kid, around nine years old, we traveled together in a show. He would bathe me in the morning and teach me how to talk to an audience. He'd say to me, "Hit 'em first with a fast gag!" He was the best. So much for Eddie Cantor.

Mel   I happen to know, George, that when you were nine years old you were an errand boy for the great singer, Enrico Caruso.

G.J.   That's right. I used to bring cigarettes and newspapers to the Metropolitan Opera House. Caruso was the greatest opera singer of them all.

Mel   I'm sure that a lot of people in the audience are curious about a gentleman who was known as, perhaps, the greatest entertainer that ever lived. Could you tell us a little bit about Al Jolson?

G.J.   Al Jolson was without question the greatest entertainer that ever lived. Remember this, we are both using a microphone so that the audience

Mel Simons and George Jessel

can hear us. Jolson was sixty-five before he needed a microphone. He sang in ballparks and theatres that seat six thousand people.

There was nobody like Jolson. He was born in Russia, you know. He came to this country when he was an infant. He was one of a kind.

Mel   I'd like to throw out a few names to you, George, and if you could comment on some of the show biz greats that you were associated with. Tell us about Sophie Tucker.

G.J.   Sophie Tucker was quite a woman. She was in a show that I wrote years ago. Before she passed away, one of the last things she requested was that she wanted me to deliver the eulogy at her funeral, which I did. She was quite a woman. And despite the fact that she was always fat and happy looking, she was a very unhappy woman. I don't think any man ever meant it when he said, "I love you." It was very sad.

Mel   How about Harry Richman?

G.J.   Harry Richman, next to Jolson, was the greatest singer of popular songs we ever had. He was a very generous guy; so much so that he died broke. I buried him, as I did Miss Tucker, and Mr. Jolson. In fact, I buried nearly everybody, but you, and you're still here, thank God!

(Laughter)

Mel   Thank God is right.

(Laughter)

Mel   I have always wanted to ask you this question, and I'm so glad that I can ask you this in person, George. As everyone knows, you starred on Broadway in *The Jazz Singer.*

G.J.   Yes. It was a stage play. I wrote a great deal of it. Then it was made into a movie by Mr. Jolson. As a matter of fact, the dialogue in the play was never in the movie. The line was, "Folks, you ain't heard nothin' yet." The rest of the movie he sang twelve songs. They didn't follow the original script at all.

If it hadn't been for Jolson being a millionaire even then, the movie would have never been made, because he put up the money. Warner Bros. had little money at the time.

George Jessel and Mel Simons

Mel   Were you ever considered for that first talkie?

G.J.   Oh, I was engaged for it, but as I said, they had no money to make it, and it was better the way they made it with Jolson.

Mel   For years you were associated, as I mentioned in the introduction, you were named by five presidents as The Toastmaster General of the United States.

G.J.   That's true.

Mel   Could you comment on your association with some of the presidents?

G.J.   Yes. Well, originally an article by Earl Wilson in the *Esquire* Magazine said that the government ought to give me that title. Earl Wilson said it. Then at a private dinner, Mr. Roosevelt, FDR, called me that. Then, later on, Harry Truman used it publicly. This was followed by Lyndon Johnson and John Kennedy. I was very, very close to Richard Nixon.

Mel   I was greatly impressed with what you showed me backstage, the present that Harry Truman gave you. Would you tell the folks about it?

G.J.   Yes. I was wounded at Vietnam, twice. Truman sent me his cane, with his initials, which I am carrying now.

Mel   George, you said that you had eight months of formal education. What have you done over the years to educate yourself?

G.J.   Having had little education as a child and traveling with a show after I left the baseball club, I had a yearning to read and learn. Since then I believe I'm one of the best well-read men ever in my business. So I am well qualified to talk about the letters of nearly all religions.

Well, Mel, I want to leave you with a poem that I dedicate to the people here in Brickman's. It's a poem that I recite when I get the opportunity on television. It's called "Old Friends," and it goes like so:

> Make new friends but keep the old
> Those are silver, these are gold
> New-made friendships, like new wine
> Age will mellow and refine.
> Friendships that have stood the test
> Of time and change, are surely best.
> Brow may wrinkle, hair turn gray,
> Friendship never knows decay.
> For 'mid old friends tried and true
> Once more we our youth renew.
> Cherish friendship in your breast
> New is good, but old is best.
> Make new friends but keep the old
> Those are silver—these are gold.

Good afternoon.

Mel   Ladies and gentlemen, one of the truly great show business legends, George Jessel.

(Applause and a standing ovation)

Milton Berle

MILTON BERLE (JULY 12, 1908-MARCH 27, 2002) was the television's first
major star—hence his nickname "Mr. Television." "Uncle Miltie"—as he was
also known to his millions of fans—was the brash host of the infinitely popular
Texaco Star Theater, which ran on the NBC network from 1948 to 1955. One
of the most prolific performers in show business, he conquered every medium
from vaudeville to movies to nightclubs.

The first time I met Milton Berle was when we did a television show together in Boston in the late 'seventies. I later had the honor of emceeing him
several times in the Catskill Mountains. Milton (or Mendel, his real name) had
an encyclopedic mind. He regaled me with story after story of the show business
greats he worked with throughout his long career. The following is a telephone
conversation I had with him on June 15, 1981.

M.B.   Hello?

Mel   Hello, Milton, it's Mel Simons.

M.B.   Which Mel Simons is this?

Mel   This is the Mel Simons who promised to send you many of your old
        radio shows.

M.B.   Oh, great, Mel. How are you?

Mel   I'm fine, thank you. I own all of your Phillip Morris radio shows.

M.B.   From what years?

Mel   Nineteen forty seven and Nineteen forty eight, I believe. In that era.

M.B.   Were those the Nat Hiken shows?

Mel   Yes. Different salutes you did every week.

M.B.   Oh, I love that.

Mel   They are all in great sound. I'll send you a bunch every week.

M.B.   You'll send them on cassette?

Mel   Yes.

M.B.   Have you got them all marked, who we did the salutes to and the dates?

Mel   Absolutely. I'll send you several shows every week.

M.B.   Great, Baby!

Mel   You did a lot of radio before you hit it big on television. How did it all begin for you on radio, both as a guest and with your own show?

M.B.   Well, the first real broadcast I was on was with Rudy Vallee.

Mel   What year was that?

M.B.   In 1928. It was called *The Fleishman Yeast Hour.* I was the first ever to do a standup on radio. Vallee introduced me, and I said to him, something like, "It's a lovely suit. Who shines it for you?"

Then I went into a monologue. It was a three-and-a-half to four-minute monologue. I was the first ever to dare in 1928 to do a monologue in front of a studio audience and on the air. I did about twenty-five weeks with Rudy Vallee.

I must admit, I was never too successful on radio. Even though the jokes were fairly good, my delivery was good, but I was more visual than I was audible. You had to see me to appreciate me.

I didn't have a distinctive voice like Fred Allen or Jack Benny. I didn't have any labels or images or identification. I would just ramble on doing monologues without having any character to it. You know what I mean?

Uncle Miltie and Mel Simons

Mel   Yes.

M.B.   So they laughed. It was all single one-liners. I didn't do stories. I did one-liners, like I do now. I never was too successful on radio, even though I did a lot of radio.

Mel   What was the next show that you were involved with?

M.B.   Let me see. Oh, I did a program called *The Gillette Community Sing.* Did you ever hear of it?

Mel   No, I'm not familiar with it at all. What year was that, Milton?

M.B.   That was in 1936. Irving Brecher wrote a lot of my material. I was the master of ceremonies. Burt Gordon, the Mad Russian, was a regular on the show. It was a forty-five minute show. We broke in in your hometown [Boston].

Mel   How long was that show on?

M.B.   The show was on for three years. Then in 1939 I was approached by Cal Tinney to be the host of a half-hour comedy show called *Stop Me If You Heard This One.*

Mel Simons with Milton Berle

People would send in jokes, and I would tell the jokes up to the punch-line. The panel I had would try to come up with the finish. If the panel was stumped, the person who sent the joke in would receive a Zenith radio. I did that show for about three years.

Then I did *The Ziegfeld Follies of the Air*. I was on that show for quite a long time with Benny Fields.

Mel   What was the year of that show, Milton?

M.B.   The year, I'm trying to think. Then I was on with Kate Smith. I did her show about fifty times. That was in the late thirties and early forties.

In 1943, I did a show sponsored by Campbell's. It was called *The Milton Berle Show*. Some of the writers I had over the years were Milt Josefsberg, Mel Shavelson, Aaron Rubin, Neil and Danny Simon, Nat Hiken, Herman Wouk. Every big comedy writer wrote for me at one time.

In 1945, I started the first telethon on radio. It was for the Heart Fund.

Mel   Was this a national hookup, the telethon?

M.B.   No, it was local. Then in 1945, I was at The Carnival Night Club in New York. I stayed for fifty-one weeks.

Besides playing there, I did many guest appearances on different radio programs. Then in 1947, I had *The Phillip Morris Show*.

Mel   Well, what about the Eversharp show? Aren't you forgetting that?

M.B.   Which one?

Mel   *Let Yourself Go.*

M.B.   Oh, yes. That was 1944

Mel   I have that marvelous show that you did with Al Jolson.

M.B.   You have that on tape too?

Mel   Yes. I'll send you that also.

M.B.   Well, *The Jolson Show,* that's a thing that always annoyed me. We did *The Jolson Show* one week talking about his life. I did the narration. Sidney Skolsky heard the show and sold it to Columbia Pictures and it became *The Jolson Story.*

Milton Berle and George Jessel

Getting back to the Phillip Morris show, it then became *The Texaco Show*. Nat Hiken was the head writer. He used to write for Fred Allen.

Then I went on television for Texaco and later *The Buick Berle Show*.

Mel What was your budget when you started *The Texaco Star Theatre?*

M.B. Fifteen thousand dollars a week. That included the guest stars, the band, the costumes, everything. We couldn't afford more.

Mel Who were your original writers on *The Texaco Show?*

M.B. There were no writers the first year. I did my monologue and the sketches that I remembered from my vaudeville days.

Mel Every show was live, right?

M.B. Oh, yes. There were no cue cards, no teleprompters. If something went wrong, or a piece of scenery would fall, I would adlib. There was no laugh machine like there is today. You saw what you got, and you got what you saw!

Mel At the beginning, you had a rating of eighty-eight!

M. B. That's because there were only eighty-eight TV sets!

Mel *The Texaco Start Theatre* was on every Tuesday night at eight o'clock. How many live shows did you do?

M.B. About a hundred and eighty live shows. Then *The Texaco Show* because *The Buick Berle Show*. Our regulars were Arnold Stang and Ruth Gilbert. Between the two shows, we were on seven and a half years.

Mel Great memories, Milton. I will have the pleasure of emceeing you next month at the Brickman Hotel.

M.B. Yes. I look forward to seeing you then.

Mel Thank you, Milton.

M.B. You're welcome, Mel. See you in a few weeks.

Willard Waterman

WILLARD LEWIS WATERMAN (AUGUST 29, 1914-FEBRUARY 2, 1995) was a highly recognizable character actor on radio, television and in movies. Although he played innumerable roles in his long career, he is best known for having succeeded Harold Peary as the title character of The Great Gildersleeve at the height of the radio show's popularity. When the show moved to television in 1955, Willard continued to play Gildersleeve. More than just one character, however, Waterman was a stage actor and singer who appeared in many Broadway shows, including Mame. On television he had memorable character parts on *Dennis the Menace*, *The Dick Van Dyke Show*, *F Troop* and *77 Sunset Strip*.

I spoke with the man behind the stentorian voice on June 26, 1986.

Mel   Willard?

W.W.   Yes.

Mel   Mel Simons calling from Boston, Massachusetts.

W.W.   How are you, Mel?

Mel   Fine. Thank you. I really appreciate your time. You are most gracious. I'd like to talk to you about your career and ask you a few questions.

W.W.   Certainly

Mel   Where are you from originally?

W.W.   Well, I was born in Madison, Wisconsin. I finally went after grade school and high school to the University of Wisconsin until my junior year, and in my junior year I was so busy working in the theatre and working in the WHA, which was the state-owned-radio station, I somehow didn't have time to attend classes, so Dean Goodnight called me in and he said, "Willard, I've heard you on the radio and I've see you at the theatre, and you seem to know what you're doing, and I think since you can't find time to attend classes, and we have a rule that you must do that, I think you better get out and see if you can make your living as an actor."

Well, it was good advice, and that was the beginning of the heyday in radio in Chicago, and so I left university in 1934, and I got involved in the beginning of the soap operas, and after a short time of breaking in and going around and pounding on agency doors and asking for auditions and a chance to work on some of the shows that were involved I got parts on a lot of the soap operas, and in fact, on the kid shows. The Tom Mixes and the Orphan Annies and the Jack Armstrongs and the Captain Midnights and many, many, many others, and I would up in Chicago doing probably 40 shows a week, usually from seven o'clock in the morning until ten, eleven o'clock at night.

The evening shows were *The First Nighter* and *Grand Hotel* and *Fifth Row Center,* and if you are a radio buff, you probably will remember a lot of these.

Mel   Of course,

W.W.   *Lights Out* and so many of the other shows that were a half-hour situation comedy.

Mel   How did you manage forty shows a week?

W.W.   Well, most of them were fifteen-minute shows, and as I say, we'd start at seven o'clock in the morning and go through the soaps, and we had an hour rehearsal and a fifteen-minute show, and sometimes you'd even do more than two fifteen-minute shows inside of an hour, an hour and a half, cutting from rehearsal to rehearsal, and it worked out to about forty shows a week.

Mel   Wow! You know, my earliest remembrance of you, Willard, was on the Tom Mix Shows.

W.W.   Yeah.

Mel   Am I correct? And I think it was Sheriff Mike Shaw.

W.W.   No. No. I played mostly villains. I did a heavy, a villain, called Diamonds. I also did a friend of Tom's called Long Bull Billy.

Willard Waterman

Photo: LICHTMAN, N.Y.C.

In those days you could do more than one character in a show. The beautiful part about radio was that you could do anything you could sound. You didn't have to look like.

Mel   Well, you know, it's interesting, Willard, the fact that you would do more than one role at the same time on *Tom Mix* and Harold Peary also did roles, and it's interesting in the respect that your voices were so similar. How did you work that?

W.W.   Well, Hal and I were both in Chicago pre-*Gildersleeve*. We worked on a lot of shows together, and when we'd go in on the rehearsal, we'd get together, and we would say, "Do you want to go high, and I'll go low?"

or "You do a dialect, and I won't," and we always changed our voices.

The beautiful part about radio was that you could change your voice. You could play anything you could sound. You didn't have to look the part.

Mel   Yes, of course.

W.W.   And the character I did on *Tom Mix* was a heavy, as I say, called Diamonds, and he was supposed to weigh 350 pounds, and the character went something like this: [Speaking in a low gravelly voice] "Now, Tom, I tell you right now, there's one thing I want to get straight. This is not a very big town, and there's not room in it for you and me together, so I'm going to stay and I guess you'd better get out!" That was Jarred Diamonds.

Mel   Oh, boy, do you bring back memories!

W. W.   And then Hal played this Hog Barrett, who was another villain, another heavy, and he played it in a rather light, sinister voice, I guess, so we could work on the same show.

Mel   Are there any other memorable roles that you recall before we get into *Gildersleeve*, other roles of certain shows that you were associated with?

W.W.   Well, I did Dad Webster on *Those Websters* for about four years.

Mel   Can you give us a little example of that, please?

W.W.   Well, he was a father and exasperated many time, and he'd get excited about what was going on, but he was a really nice guy underneath, and I enjoyed it.

I played that for about four years. Two years in Chicago and then as a matter of fact I came to the West Coast with that show. We did one show on one Sunday in Chicago, and the next Sunday we did it from out here. The whole cast caravanned out from Chicago and got together out here.

Jamie Webb and Eddie Firestone, Jr. and Connie Crowder was Ma Webster, and well, oh, gosh—

Mel   I'm bringing back memories to you too, I see.

W.W.   Yeah. And as usual, my memory plays me false on these things. Hartzell, who did the part in—Uncle Fletcher. He played an uncle in—(long pause)—

Mel   How about some of the soap operas that you did? Any come to mind?

W.W.   Well, I did *Road of Life.* I did *Stepmother.* At one time or another I was on every—*Guiding Light.* Betty Lou Gerson and I played the leads on *Guiding Light* for a number of years in Chicago, and then when the show moved out here to the West Coast we continued out here for a couple of years, and I don't think there was any soap opera that originated in – *The Bachelor Children.* These are coming back off the top of my head. But I don't think there was any soap opera that originated in Chicago during those years that I didn't do at some time.

          I'd do a character that would run maybe two or three weeks, six months or something like that, and then, of course, as I say, I'd go down to the kid shows in the afternoon, and *Tom Mix* quite regularly, and *Captain Midnight.*

Mel   Who did you play on Captain *Midnight?*

W.W   Well, nothing—no character that was notable. I'd play whatever happened to come up in the script that day or that week or whatever it was. I didn't have any regular character.

Mel   Now, Willard, I think that people know and love you best, of course, as *The Great Gildersleeve,* and I believe that Gildersleeve was perhaps the first spin-off ever on radio where Gildy was a character of Fibber *McGee and Molly.*

W.W.   That's absolutely right.

Mel   And then branched out in 1941 with Harold Peary.

W.W.   That's right.

Mel   Now, could you bring us up to I believe it was either 'fifty or 'fifty-one—am I correct?—when you replaced Hal Peary as Gildy.

W.W.   'Fifty.

Mel   And could you tell us the story behind that.

W.W.   Well, Hal started in forty-one and played it until 1950, and in 1950 was the year that CBS was raiding all the NBC talent. Benny, Phil Harris, quite a few of the NBC stars went over to CBS, and Hal's agent at that time sold him to CBS, put him under contract, expecting to deliver the show, the *Gildersleeve* show, which was on for Kraft.

Unfortunately—Well, fortunately for me, I guess Kraft did not want to change networks, so Hal was then already under contract to CBS, and it became a question of replacing Hal on Gildersleeve, and so Frank Pitman, who was directing at the time, called me, and it has become fairly well known that there was a great similarity of voice between Hal and myself, and so he called me and asked me if I would come in and read for Andy White and John Elliott and Paul West, who were the writers.

The thing was they couldn't make up their minds whether they wanted to go with a sound-alike or whether they wanted to go with an entirely different character, and so he thought that it might be good for me to come in and read, so I could make my mind up whether I wanted to do it or not, because I was not really very eager to do anything like that, because I was sort of taking my career in my hands, and I could have gone down the drain with it.

Mel   Yes.

W.W.   And so I went in and I read the script the boys had written, and it was written so beautifully. I mean, the script was so much Gildersleeve that I found that I didn't have to do an imitation of any kind. I just played the character the way it was and used my own voice, which was a little bit heavier in quality than Hal's, but by playing the character I pushed it up a level, so it worked right into the Gildersleeve character beautifully.

I didn't ever feel I had to do an imitation. In fact, one thing I did not do, and this is hard for people to realize, because a lot of people see me today and they say, "You were Gildersleeve. Let me hear you laugh," because they were thinking about Hal's laugh. That hee hee hee laugh, which I didn't use. I used what the writers' used to call the Gildersleeve social chuckle. That heh heh heh heh.

(Mel laughs)

W.W.   But I didn't use the laugh that Hal did, because we did a show in Chicago before either *Gildersleeve* was known at all called *Thanks You, Stusia* with Bernadine Flynn, Templeton Fox, and Mark Harvey and a lot of other people that you—names that you remember from old radio.

Mel   Surely

W.W.   And he used that laugh in a character called "Professor Rollo," and he also uses it as Gildersleeve, so I just figured I wouldn't use that, because that was sort of a signature, and it was truly a signature with Gildersleeve, because people remembered that even though I did it for nine years without using the laugh. I laughed, of course, but I tried not to use that *particular* laugh.

        I did all the diphthongs, the things that were part of the character, the hees and the hohs, and the melahs, and all those things, but I didn't use the laugh.

Mel   That's wonderful. And *The Great Gildersleeve* went off radio what year, Willard?

W.W.   Nineteen fifty-eight, 'fifty-*nine* actually.

Mel   I can recall you starring in *The Great Gildersleeve* on television.

W.W.   That's right.

Mel   But it was not the same premise as when you did it on radio.

W.W.   No.

Mel   Why did they change it? Why did the TV people change it when it was so successful all those years on radio?

W.W.   Well, there are probably a lot of reasons for it, but I think one of the prime reasons was that the person that NBC picked to produce the show, they'd never heard the radio show and didn't take any trouble to find out much about it, and he had an idea that Gildersleeve was a skirt chaser, which was far from being true, because Gildy had an eye for the ladies, sure, but if they turned around, he ran.

Mel   Yes. I can remember that.

W.W.   And so I spent the first twenty-six weeks of the – We only did thirty-nine films, which is one year's product. I spent the first twenty-six weeks chasing big-breasted broads that I would rather not have been chasing.

Mel   Yes.

W.W.   There were a lot of other things too. We missed the Leroy character.

Mel   Well, you know it's interesting, that leads into my next question, Willard. I'd like to throw out some of the names of the characters that appeared with you on *Gildersleeve*, and if you could comment on them.

        Let's start with Walter Tetley.

W.W.   Well, Walter Tetley, there was no other. He was so wonderful. Nobody could read lines the way Walter did. Of course, Walter was not really a youngster. When he died a year or so ago he was, oh, about sixty, I guess, but he had played youngsters so long and he knew that his voice never had changed, and he was so proficient in playing that kind of comedy that he just couldn't reproduce it on television.

Mel   He had a marvelous flair for comedy, as I remember it.

W.W.   Absolutely.

Mel   His timing was impeccable.

W.W.   That's right. Excellent.

Mel   Tell us about Peavey.

W.W.   *Peavey?*

Mel   Mr. Peavey.

W.W.   That was Dick Legrand.

Mel   Yes.

W.W.   And there again there just was no other Peavey. Unfortunately, just before we began to do the television series Dick had an illness, and he was laid up for quite a while. As a matter of fact, we had to go out to his home to tape his scenes in the radio show.

Mel   Now, he did not appear as Peavey on TV?

W.W.   No. No. He didn't. A very fine actor and a good friend of mine, Forrest Lewis played Peavey, but he just was not Peavey. That's all, the Peavey that we knew so well and was always in the drugstore every time Gildy walked in, and his favorite line of course, "Well, now, I wouldn't say that."

Mel   Oh, people would laugh just when he used to say that. You knew exactly what he was going to say, and people laughed each and every week.

W.W.   Oh, that's—

Mel   Judge Hooker.

W.W.   Judge Hooker.

Mel   Horace, I believe.

W.W.   Yeah, He was the one—as I say, he looked like an old goat. He had a white mustache and white hair, and when he'd get a little upset, that hair would stand up, and he looked just like an old goat. Horace was just perfect for the part, and there again, the producer who we had for the television series never even interviewed him at all, so we didn't have a chance to have him on the show, and we missed a lot.

Mel   That's too bad. Another lady that I loved, and I believe she was also on the TV version was Birdie.

W.W.   Oh, Lillian Randolph.

Mel   Has she passed away?

W.W.   Yes. About a year ago, unfortunately. She was so wonderful. She just was the head of the family, that's all.

Mel   Yes. Was Lillian Randolph related to Amanda Randolph?

W.W.   Oh, yes, yes.

Mel   Sisters?

W.W.   They were sisters.

Mel   Yes. I always thought that in my mind, but I never knew it.

W.W.   Well, they both used to be on the *Amos & Andy Show* after *Amos & Andy* did the half-hour version.

Mel   Yes, I believe one played Mama and the other was Madame Queen?

W.W.   Lillian played Madame Queen, and Amanda played Kingfish's mother-in-law.

Mel   Yes. Mama

W.W.   Yes. Mama, Mama.

Mel   Great character.

W.W.   Yeah.

Mel   How many different gals played Marjorie? It seems to me there was more than one.

W.W.   Only two. Lorene Tuttle.

Mel   Oh, Lorene Tuttle, who just passed away?

W.W.   She just passed away—[she] originated it, and then Mary Lee Robb played it all the time that I did it, and I guess she'd taken it over sometime after the first four or five years of the show.

Mel   Then, of course, there was your perennial girlfriend, Leila Ramson.

W.W.   Yeah, that was Shirley Mitchell.

Mel   Tell us about Shirley.

W.W.   Well, she's a wonderful gal. She did the show, did the character to begin with, and then she got married, and she left the show—and I'm trying to think of the gal who took her place—but then she came back at the same time that I took over the show she was back playing Leila, and she was wonderful in it. She was the *southernest* Southern girl you've ever heard.

Mel   "Throckmorton!"

W.W.   "Throckmorton!"

Mel   Always a wonderful, wonderful show.

W.W.   Yeah.

Mel   I hope you will write a book. Anything in the works on that? Thinking of doing it?

W.W.   Well, everybody says I should write a book.

Mel   You were on so many shows. You have a lot. It would be a great thing to have.

W.W.   I don't have the kind of stick-to-it-iveness that puts the seat of the pants in the seat of the chair and writes the book. If I could sit down and talk a book. In fact, I've thought seriously sometimes about sitting down with a tape machine and putting down all these remembrances, but I need somebody to jog my memory sometimes.

        We get into a group of old radio people, which I do occasionally. There's an outfit out here called the Pacific Pioneer Broadcasters, and we get together every other month for a luncheon, and there are 750 or more, and we get to yakking about radio, and somebody will say, "Do you remember what happened when?" and I say, "Oh, yeah. I remember now." And it would be wonderful to have somebody jog my memory on things like that.

Mel   I hope you will, and the other thing is you're on the West Coast, aren't you?

W.W.   Yes, I am on the West Coast.

Mel   I have to tell you that as a youngster that *The Great Gildersleeve* was one of my favorite programs, and I enjoyed many hours listening to it, and I want to thank you for all the enjoyment you've given me over the years.

W.W.   Well, thank you. The wonderful thing about radio, I think, was that it was a thing that the whole family could join in.

Mel   That's right.

W.W.   The whole family of the kids and the older people would get together on Wednesday night to listen to *Gildersleeve* and on Tuesday night for *Fibber* and Sunday night for *Benny*, and it was a wonderful experience for everybody. That's the way I felt about it anyway.

Mel   It was clean, wholesome entertainment. You didn't worry about sex and violence the way you do today.

W.W.   Thank you.

Mel   Did you have any *Gildersleeve* shows that were your favorites, that you really enjoyed doing or stand out in your memory as, you know, as being very good? You said that the script that you read for the audition was so well written and you enjoyed it.

W.W.   Yeah

Mel   Did you have any others that you remember?

W.W.   Well, I really enjoyed every one I ever did.

Mel   That's nice.

W.W.   None of them stand out. In fact, I have tapes of the first four years that I did, and they're very memorable because of the fact that I was on tenterhooks as to whether or not I could do it or not, and fortunately it worked out and came off very well, and I enjoyed that first season particularly.

         But even in the later years when we were taping, which we didn't do for many, many years, I enjoyed almost all of them. I loved a lot of the shows I did with Walter. I mean, the Gildy/Leroy relationship was a wonderful, wonderful thing, and I really enjoyed "Leroy"-ing my nephew, above all.

Mel   You've done different mediums. I know you've done television and radio, and they tell me you've also done stage. I get the feeling that you really love radio. Was it your favorite medium to work in, or did you prefer stage?

W.W.   Well, it was certainly—radio was a wonderful medium to work in, and I enjoyed every bit I ever did of it. I didn't really get involved in that until later in my career, the stage. I fortunately did two years of *How to Succeed in Business Without Really Trying* in the national company, the Rudy Vallee part, and then of course I did *Mame* with Angela Lansbury.

         In fact, I was in Boston with that before we opened on Broadway. I played the banker, Babcock, and I did that for two years with Angela, and then two more years on Broadway after that, and as I say, I had done a lot of stage work in Wisconsin at university, and then I got out of it except for some summer stock down at La Jolla, and then in the later years I got into and I spent, oh, from 'sixty-two or 'three until almost 'seventy-something in New York. I was fourteen years in New York and did an awful lot of stage work, and I enjoyed that, too.

| Mel | You sound like you enjoyed acting and you've enjoyed everything you've done. |

Mel   You sound like you enjoyed acting and you've enjoyed everything you've done.

W.W.   Well, it's been a great life. I hope it isn't over yet.

Mel   That's nice to be able to say, that you've enjoyed it, and it's been great, and I'm happy for you.

W.W.   Thank you.

Mel   Incidentally, Willard, I had the pleasure of seeing you in *Mame* in New York City, and you were outstanding.

W.W.   Thank you. Thank you.

Mel   There were two individuals that I have rather lost track of that I think you probably have worked with over the years, and I wonder if you know where they've been. One of them is Parker Fennelly, who played "Titus Moody" on Fred Allen. I lost track of him in New York. And the other one is, of course, Jim Jordan, the great Fibber McGee, who I think is still living.

W.W.   Yes, he is. I didn't know Fennelly, because he was primarily in New York, and the radio I did was either Chicago or on the West Coast, but Jim I do know, and of course, I knew him in Chicago when they started *Fibber*, and I see him quite regularly now.

As I said earlier, there's an outfit called the Pacific Pioneer Broadcasters, which I belong to, and they have meetings during the winter every other month, and I usually go down to L.A. for that. In fact, the last— not the last one, but the one before the last was their twentieth anniversary of PPB, and I was on the dais with Jim, and Lorene Tuttle, she was there. Unfortunately, she has passed away—and so many of the others, including Don Ameche. We were all original members of PPB, and so we got to talk at the meetings.

Mel   You also have another little person that used to instigate you when you were on TV, Jay North, who was *Dennis the Menace*.

W.W.   *Dennis the Menace*, yes.

Mel   And you played the grocer.

W.W.   I was the grocer, Mr. Quigley, yeah.

Mel   And on that same episode that I saw just recently, Joseph Kearns was in it with you.

W.W.   Oh, yes.

Mel   And there were two fantastic radio personalities right there on the same set. It was terrific to see both of you together.

W.W.   Well, thank you. Joe was a wonderful guy, and we mention him around here. We haven't for a long time, but he was a great actor and a nice guy.

Mel -   Well, Willard, you have been great for the past thirty, thirty-five minutes, and I thank you immensely. I will send you the tapes that I told you about this morning. I'll get them off.

W.W.   I appreciate that.

Mel   Sure. You'll get them in a few days, plus a copy of this interview.

W.W.   Oh, that would be nice.

Mel   It has been a delight and a joy talking to you.

W.W.   Well, thank you, Mel.

Mel   Thank you, Willard, once again. Good-bye and God bless.

W.W.   Good-bye, and God bless you.

Mel   Thank you.

W.W.   Good-bye.

Mel   Bye-Bye.

Morey Amsterdam

MOREY AMSTERDAM (DECEMBER 14, 1908-OCTOBER 27, 1996) was known affectionately as "The Human Joke Machine." (I used to throw out any topic and Morey would be ready with a first-rate joke.) He began his career in vaudeville in 1922 and went on to make audiences laugh for decades. Often at his side was his cello, which he played expertly between jokes. A songwriter as well, he wrote his theme song, "Yuk-a-Puk" and "Rum and Coca-Cola." The latter song was recorded by the Andrews Sisters and was number one on *Your Hit Parade* for ten weeks. Morey achieved television immortality in his signature role of comedy writer Buddy Sorrell on *The Dick Van Dyke Show*. I talked with the affable comic on March 25, 1992.

Mel   Hi, Morey. It's Mel Simons calling from Boston.

M.A.   How are you, Mel?

Mel   Fine, thank you. Morey, you are one of the most lovable comedians in the history of show business. This morning I was playing your lovely song *Yuk-A-Puk*. Is that your theme song, Morey?

M.A.   It's a funny thing about that song. There's a whole big story about how I happened to invent it. You know, I've written a lot of hit songs. I wrote "Rum and Coca-Cola," "Why Did I Ever Leave Wyoming?"—a lot of those kind of things.

        That song came out of nowhere, because, you know, I'm a cello player. And the background for the piano accompanist goes up and down, and I do ask my piano player to play and I started to adlib "Yuk-A-Puk."

        I never thought anything more about it. Then I started getting letters from people saying, "Dear Yuk-A-Puk." I did my first album and I needed another song, so I wrote "Yuk-A-Puk," and it's stuck with me ever since.

Mel   And that has become your theme song. When you entertain, I know the band always brings you on with that song.

M.A.   Yes—either that or 'The Dick Van Dyke Theme.' I wrote the lyrics for the Van Dyke theme, by the way.

Mel   Oh, I didn't know you did the Van Dyke theme. I was aware that you wrote one of the biggest selling records of all time, "Rum and Coca-Cola." Tell us about your writing that song. How did that come about?

M.A.   Well, I was going overseas during the war. I went to Africa, India, China, Burma. I made all the theatres during the war, entertaining. We got to Trinidad and I just couldn't wait to get there. I said, "Oh, boy, I want to hear those calypso singers that I heard so much about."

Well, I didn't know that the calypsos have what they call a tent season. They are only there at certain times during the year. Well, we get down there, and sure enough, they weren't there. So I thought to myself, *Well, I've got to entertain the guys with something unusual*—and I got the idea for "Rum and Coca-Cola." So I wrote it, and I wrote 105 dirty verses. It's the truth. Anything to entertain the troops.

When I came back to the states, there was a girl singer going into a nightclub in New York. She needed a novelty song, so I wrote a couple of special lyrics for her. She got rave reviews in the newspapers.

Then I ran into the Andrews Sisters. They said that they were recording three days later. They wanted to do "Rum and Coca-Cola." They did it, and it became one of the biggest record sellers of all time.

Mel   Sure did. How many records did "Rum and Coca-Cola" sell?

M.A.   Well, the Andrews Sisters' record, when it first came out, they sold over five million records. Jack Kapp, who was the head of Decca Records, said to me, "We could have sold another 10 million, but we can't get the shellac."

It was during the war, so that was the thing. But since then, now it's becoming a hit in Europe again. You never know with a song! I wrote "Why Did I Ever Leave Wyoming?" I wrote it as a cowboy song. It's now the state song of Wyoming.

Morey Amsterdam with Mel Simons

Mel   You're quite an accomplished songwriter and musician as well. I want
       to go back to the very beginning, Morey. Did you always want to do
       comedy when you were a little fellow?

M.A.   I was never the funny kid at home. I was never the funny kid at school,
       or anything else. I was a serious concert cellist. My brother went out
       with a vaudeville act in those days, and he came back a year later, and he
       was a straight man for the comic in the act.

The comic got sick, and he recruited me, and I had never been on the stage in my life. My brother said, "Are you a little nervous?" I said, "Yes." He said, "Never be nervous." I said, "What do you mean, 'Never be nervous'?" He said, "All those people out there paid to get in, and you're seeing the show for nothing."

Mel   You know what I always remember you telling me years ago, Morey, that Al Capone, the famous gangster, used to send for you.

M.A.   My first nightclub job, he owned the club in Chicago. This is a true story. He was introduced to me as Al Brown. They said, "He's a furniture dealer in Indianapolis," or something like that.

          And after about six weeks, I found out he was Capone. So I said to him, "Are you Al Capone?" He said, "That's right." I said, "I didn't know you were in the cement business."

Mel   I hope he laughed!

M.A.   Well, instead of getting mad, he got hysterical! And from then on, I was his boy. He treated me like his kid brother.

          He had a little club called The Greyhound where he had living quarters in the back. He'd send the guys to pick me up. I was working at another club that he owned. He would send the guys, you know, with the crooked noses to pick me up. He'd say, "Bring the cello along."

          So I'd go out there and I'd play these Italian tarantellas and sing with the cello, and he'd cook for me. He used to make spaghetti and meatballs. I am probably the only guy in the world that ever had Al Capone cook for them.

Mel   That's beautiful. So obviously, you got along very well with Al Capone.

M.A.   He took me out on his yacht fishing and everything else. He was very good to me.

          I started in radio when I was ten years old. I was a boy soprano in San Francisco. As a matter of fact, I had a very high voice. In school, they made me sit with the girls. Then when I began to enjoy it, my voice changed.

          I did a lot of radio. I was with *Al Pearce and His Gang* for five years … we were the most popular daytime show in radio.

Mel   Sure, a famous name, Al Pearce. Tell me about some of the early television shows that you did.

M.A.   Well, I started on television right here on KHJ, which was the first franchised television station in America. In those days, they must have had, maybe, 70 TV sets in all of California.

I was doing experimental television. In those days, the lights were absolutely unbearable. It was so hot, and the makeup that you put on was white. Everybody looked like Marcel Marceau.

Then I went on to many other shows. I had my own shows. I had *The Morey Amsterdam Show,* which was *The Golden Goose Café.* I had that for three years. Art Carney was a waiter on that show. Jacqueline Suzanne was the cigarette girl.

We had a nightclub setting. People actually thought we were doing the show from a nightclub. They used to call in for reservations! I've been in just about every branch of the entertainment business that there is.

Mel   I think that most people remember Morey Amsterdam from *The Dick Van Dyke Show.*

M.A.   Well, that had the biggest audience, because by that time, television was really widespread, and almost everyone had a television set. I was on that show for five years. I must tell you, we were really a happy family. We all got along great. We all had fun doing it.

People like Danny Thomas, Jack Benny, Lucille Ball, used to walk in and we were rehearsing, but we were probably telling each other jokes. They said, "How do you idiots ever get a show on the air?"

Mel   How did you get that role, Morey? I mean, you were perfect for it. I really can't see anyone else doing it.

M.A.   They were all sitting around at a meeting. First of all, Carl Reiner did the show by himself. And I have a copy of the original show with Carl playing the part that Dick Van Dyke wound up with. A kid by the name of Morty Gunty played the part I was supposed to play.

And they all looked at it and decided that they had a good show, but they had the wrong people in it. Then they started casting it. They had everybody cast except Buddy, the guy who worked in the office writing jokes. So they're all sitting around talking about it. They said, "We need a guy who's a comedian, who knows the comedy business, who's a writer," and so and so. And Rose Marie was sitting there, whom I've known since she was twelve years old. She's my daughter's Godmother. She said, "What about Morey Amsterdam?" So Carl

Reiner picks up the phone. I was living in Yonkers, New York, at the time. I was digging my car out of the snow. He said, "You want to come out here and do a show with us?" He said, "When can you leave?" I said, "In about ten minutes!" And that was it.

Mel   You know what I remember about *The Dick Van Dyke Show*, Morey. You quit while you were on top.

M.A.   Well, I'll tell you, that was really a bad decision, I felt. We all did, because the show was in the top five for the five years it was on. It was a mistake.

Dick Van Dyke's manager figured he's going to get him a couple of movies and stuff, which he did. And outside of *Mary Poppins*, I never cared for any of them, and I don't think Dick did, either.

Sheldon Leonard, who was the producer of the show, was absolutely furious. He read about it in one of the TV magazines. He didn't even know we were going to go off the air at the end of the season.

But everybody was very upset. In those days they didn't have spin offs, or Rose Marie and I would have done one. Rosie and I are very good friends. I've written everything she's ever done since she's about twelve years old.

Mel   Do you still have any sort of a relationship with the [actors] on the show?

M.A.   Oh, sure. We meet all the time. We had a big birthday party for Dick not long ago. Mary flew in from New York. All of us were there, with the exception, of course, of Richard Deacon, who had passed away.

We've always had a very close feeling between us. I must tell you one thing. We all get along beautifully. There was no temperament. It was a fun show to do. We looked forward to working together every day.

Mel   That's exactly the way it came off, Morey. I always enjoyed you on that show. Your lines, your adlibbing was just magnificent.
Now tell us about Morey Amsterdam today.

M.A.   Well, I come from a musical family. I was groomed to be a concert cellist. All my family are musicians. I'm the black sheep! I'm the one making money!

Mel   You're still working? Still doing club dates in concert?

M.A.   Oh, yeah. I work all over the world. You know the Van Dyke show plays all over the world. I've seen myself, so far, in about seven different languages!

Mel   What's your first love, Morey? Is it music or is a comedy?

M.A.   Well, you know, I've been successful in so many different mediums. People say to me, "What do you like best?" And I say, "I'm like the guy in *Finian's Rainbow.*" He said, "When I'm not near the girl I love, I love the girl I'm near."

        Whatever I am doing at the moment is the one that I like the best.

Mel   Well, Morey, it has been so much fun talking to you.

M.A.   I wanna tell you, I am well acquainted with your city. Years ago, I played in The Latin Quarter. I played The Oval Room. I played Blinstrubs. I've got a lot of friends all over Massachusetts.

Mel   Everybody loves you.

M.A.   Well, I'm a very lucky fella. I always say, I'm the happiest fella I ever met.

Mel   It comes across. It always came across. Whenever I saw you perform in person or on television.

M.A.   Well, I like people, and I've got a wonderful family. My health has been good. I must tell you something. I was in Florida doing a show this past December. Some woman in the audience yelled up at me, "How old are you?" I said, "This year I'll be 83." She said, "You don't look it." I said, "You know why? Because I very seldom come to Florida." That was the end of the question.

Mel   You are one of the show business greats.

M.A.   Thank you, Mel. Incidentally, we were at a party the other night with George Burns. I love him. He's a very dear guy. I had a blood clot on my leg last year. I was in the hospital for a couple of days. George calls me. He said, "What are you doing in the hospital?" I said, "I'll tell you, George, there was a man who was very, very sick. He couldn't make it, so I'm filling in." He said, "Oh, you're crazy," and he hung up!

Mel   I wish you many more years of entertaining, making people happy.

M.A. Well, that's the main deal. I'm having a wonderful time, as I said. I'm writing my autobiography. I mentioned that to some idiot the other night, and he said, "Who you writing about?" I said, "It's about me!" He said, "When will it be finished?" I said, "I hope not for a long time!" The book will be called *I Remember Me.*

Mel I really look forward to that book, Morey.

M.A. Well, don't just look forward to it, Mel. *Buy it* when it comes out.

Mel That's a promise. Morey Amsterdam, thank you so much. It has been a pleasure talking to you.

M.A. Thank you very much, Mel. Be well, and save your money. Someday it may be worth something.

Mel Thanks, Morey. Bye-bye.

M.A. Bye-bye.

Clayton Moore

No one needs to ask "Who was that masked man?" He was Jack Carlton Moore (September 14, 1914-December 28, 1999), the actor known to a generation of television fans as The Lone Ranger. Arriving in Hollywood in the late 1930s, Jack played in bit roles and worked as a stunt man. Around 1940 producer Edward Small convinced the aspiring actor to adopt the stage name "Clayton" Moore. With this new moniker, Moore began turning up in B-westerns and cliffhangers for Republic Studios. In 1949 he received the role by which he will always be remembered. He was briefly replaced by John Hart in 1954 when he had a salary dispute with the producers of the show. Fortunately, an agreement was reached and Clayton returned to his rightful role until the series' end in 1957.

I had the honor of interviewing this true hero on March 25, 1992. So—Return with us now to those thrilling days of yesteryear …

Mel   What a great thrill to meet and interview a gentleman that so many of us grew up with, television's Lone Ranger, Clayton Moore. Welcome Clayton.

C.M.   Well, good morning, Mel. How are you doing?

Mel   I'm doing fine. Thank you for taking a few moments of your time to spend with me.

C.M.   Well, it's my pleasure, Mel. Let me welcome you with my traditional greeting of Kemo Sabe!

Mel   Kemo Sabe! I think Kemo Sabe means "faithful friend."

C.M.   That's right.

Mel   And Tonto used to say that to you.

C.M.   That's correct.

Mel   Clayton, before we talk about *The Lone Ranger*, I am such a fan and admirer of yours, I want to talk about the serials. Because before you became television's The Lone Ranger you were really the king of serials at Republic Pictures.

Clayton Moore and Jay Silverheels as the Lone Ranger and Tonto

C.M.   That's correct, [in] 1942.

Mel   Can you tell me how you began in the movies?

C.M.   At Republic?

Mel   Yes.

C.M.   Let's see, my first picture was *Tuxedo Junction*. The second picture at Republic in 1942 was—We're going back a good many years, Mel. That would be *The Crimson Ghost*.

Mel   That serial is a classic!

C.M.   Those were fun days, let me tell you. Fourteen and fifteen episodes per serial.

Mel   How many serials did you make altogether, Clayton?

C.M.   There were so many, I can't remember.

Mel   I can imagine. Is there one serial that, perhaps, sticks out in your mind as your favorite?

C.M.   Well, let me see. To be honest with you, Mel, I just enjoyed working in them all. I don't really think I have a favorite. I just liked them all.

Mel   You were the king of the serials in the 1940's. How did you become television's Lone Ranger?

C.M.   Well, I was picked out of a number of men for the part of The Lone Ranger by George W. Trendle and Fran Striker, who was the writer and the producer of the radio show. That was 1949.

Mel   How many years was *The Lone Ranger* on television before you went into reruns?

C.M.   Well, we started in '49 and finished shooting in 1956. I made 169 TV shows and two feature-length motion pictures.

Mel   You know, Clayton, other cowboys are liked and admired, but The Long Ranger is loved. You are genuinely loved, not only as a person, but as a character, The Lone Ranger.

I always wondered—did you do your own stunts?

C.M.   I did all the horse work in the show. I really enjoy riding horses and working with horses. There were times that Jay Silverheels and myself were doubled at times.

Mel   Did you have the same horse? Was it the same Silver all those years?

C.M.   Well, I had two Silvers.

Mel   Tell me about the two Silvers.

C.M.   The last Silver that I had was an Arabic horse. He was a big horse. He weighed 1,250 pounds.

Mel   I assume the first Silver died, and then you replaced him with the second Silver.

C.M.   Yes, he died. But he lived a good long time. The second Silver was 34 years old, and he died in 1973.

Mel   Jay Silverheels was Tonto, if I'm correct.

C.M.   Right. A full-blooded Mohawk Indian.

Mel   What type of relationship did you have with Jay Silverheels?

C.M.   We were good friends. After we finished shooting the series we stayed the best of friends.

Mel   You were a wonderful duo. The best cowboy and sidekick I can ever think of.

C.M.   Thank you, Mel. As a matter of fact, Jay, as a full-blooded Mohawk Indian, was busy on the Six Nations Reservation in Branford, Canada. When he was a little guy he came to the United States of America and made this country his own.

Mel   Had Jay done any acting prior to becoming Tonto?

C.M.   Yes. He worked in pictures doing stunts and as an actor, small parts. Jay was perfect for the part of Tonto. As a matter of fact, they didn't look at any other Indians in the motion picture business except one man and that was Jay Silverheels.

Mel   Sure. He was perfect. And his wonderful horse, of course, was Scout. I remember Dan Reid, your nephew, and his horse Victor. Who played Dan Reid on the TV show?

C.M.   A fellow by the name of Chuck Courtney.

Mel   Is Chuck Courtney in the business today?

C.M.   I think he's doing a little writing and directing.

Mel   When *The Lone Ranger* ended, did it go into reruns immediately?

C.M.   Yes.

Mel   And it still is on reruns all over the country; isn't it, Clayton?

C.M.   To the best of my knowledge, yes, Mel.

Mel   You know, you are and always will be The Lone Ranger. To me, the worst thing I ever saw in movies was the recent movie *The Lone Ranger*. They had another actor portray The Lone Ranger, and I can't begin to tell you what a lousy movie it was.

C.M.   Well, let's just say that they tried very hard, and everybody did their best to do a good job.

Mel   It just didn't make it, Clayton. Are you still doing personal appearances?

C.M.   No. I kind of laid off a little bit. Every now and then I will do a personal appearance, but not too often.

Mel   Clayton, is there any special legacy that you would like to leave to your many viewers who enjoyed you so much?

C.M.   Yes—"The Lone Ranger Creed." I'll do it for you at the end of the interview.

Mel   Brace Beemer played the Lone Ranger on radio for many years. The Lone Ranger started on radio, I think, in 1933.

C.M.   That's correct.

Mel   Did you ever meet or speak with Brace Beemer?

C. M.   No, I never had the pleasure and the honor to meet Brace Beemer. George Trendle, of course, the producer, and Fran Striker, the writer, I knew very well.

Mel   I'll tell you something you used to do that I always enjoyed. Do you remember many times you would disguise yourself as perhaps an older gentlemen? In other words, you would do other characters to surprise the bad guys!

C.M.   Yes, that's correct. They were written into the show, of course.

Mel   Exactly. Any special fond memories of some of the characters you played on the show?

C.M.   I liked "The Old-Timer" the best. I kind of played him for comedy.

Mel   Yes, you did. And you did it so well, and you did it on several occasions, if I'm not mistaken.

C.M.   Yes. We did about six or seven Old-Timers. More than that, I guess. It's a little difficult to remember.

Mel   Clayton, what do you do now in the way of exercise? I know that you were a jogger. I know that you were an avid swimmer at one time. Do you still do both?

C.M.   As much as possible. Old Kemo Sabe here is getting along in years. We take it easy.

Mel   One last question, Clayton. Would you recite "The Long Ranger Creed"?

C.M.   Sure.

> "I believe that to have a friend.
> A man must be one.
>
> "That all men are created equal
> And that everyone has within himself
> the power to make this a better world.

"That God put the firewood there
but that every man
must gather and light it himself.

"In being prepared
physically, mentally, and morally
to fight when necessary
for that which is right.
"That a man should make the most
of what equipment he has.

"That 'This government,
of the people, by the people
and for the people' shall live always.

"That men should live by
the rule of what is best
for the greatest number.

"That sooner or later…
somewhere…somehow…
we must settle with the world
and make payment for what we have taken.

"That all things change but truth,
and that truth alone, lives on forever.

"In my Creator, my country, my fellow man."

Mel, that's "The Lone Ranger Creed."

Mel   That's absolutely beautiful, Clayton. I can think of no nicer way to end
this interview. It has been an honor and a privilege to speak to you,
Clayton. Thank you so much.

C.M.   Thank you, Mel. Nice talking to you. A hearty "Hi Ho, Silver!"—
Adios, Kemo Sabe.

Mel   *Adios*. Bye-bye.

Sheldon Leonard

Sheldon Leonard

SHELDON LEONARD BERSHAD (FEBRUARY 22, 1907-JANUARY 10, 1997) was a pioneering television producer, director, writer and actor. Apprenticing on Broadway in the 1930s in his native New York City, he soon became an accomplished stage actor. He used that training (and his Brooklyn accent) to good effect in Hollywood Films, including the classics *To Have and Have Not* and *It's a Wonderful Life*—and on radio, most memorably (to me) as "the tout" on *The Jack Benny Program*. In the 1950s and '60s the name Sheldon Leonard was most associated with the production side of television. He produced the successful situation comedies starring Danny Thomas, Andy Griffith and Dick Van Dyke, as well as the ground-breaking series, *I Spy*, starring Robert Culp and Bill Cosby. His autobiography, *And the Show Goes On*, was published in 1995.

I interviewed this show business veteran on my radio show on March 25, 1993.

S.L.   Hello?

Mel   Sheldon?

S.L.   Yes.

Mel   Mel Simons calling from Boston.

S.L.   Yes, sir.

Mel   How are you?

S.L.   Very well, thank you.

Mel   If I may start at the very beginning: Where were you born?

S.L.   In New York City, 102nd Street and Fifth Avenue.

Mel   So, this is a real New York accent that you have.

S.L.   That's right. At Mt. Sinai Hospital, 102nd Street and Fifth Avenue, New York.

Mel   Now, a lot of people, Sheldon, think you got your start in show business on radio, but I think you got your start on Broadway. Am I correct?

S.L.   You're correct, and the others are wrong. Indeed, I was on Broadway. I was on Broadway for ten years, through the 'thirties.

Mel   Tell us about it. Tell us some of the shows you did.

S.L.   *Having Wonderful Time, Kiss the Boys Goodbye, Three Men on a Horse, Margin for Error,* all very successful shows. They filled out a ten-year period during which I was very consistently employed in the legitimate theatre on Broadway.

Mel   Basically that's the decade of the thirties we're talking.

S.L.   That's right.

Mel   Now, after Broadway, what came next, motion pictures for you or radio?

S.L.   No. Motion pictures came—Hollywood. Metro-Goldwyn-Mayer offered me a shot at a picture with Myrna Loy and Bill Powell, one of the—

Mel   *Thin Man?*

S.L.   —early *Thin Man* pictures, and I came to California to do that, and after doing a return to Broadway to do *Margin for Error*, but then the demand for me was created by my appearance in the Metro picture, the *Thin Man* picture, and they were very attractive demands, and they lured me back to California.

Mel   What type of a character did you play in that *Thin Man* movie?

S.L.   I played a mysterious sort of threatening figure. I was the heavy, as they call it, and I was the one—the *Thin Man* pictures were all mysteries, as you may remember.

Mel   Yes, of course.

S.L.   But I was the one who was initially suspected of the crime that created the basis for the particular story, and that was a red herring. I was innocent of that, but that was my function in the picture, to misdirect attention.

Mel   Now, as far as your career on radio, of course, you have gone in so many directions both as an actor, as a writer, producer, director, how did it start on radio? Was Benny your first radio program?

S.L.   No. My first radio show, a friend of mine was writing a show for Harry Einstein, "Parkyakarkus" —

Mel   He's from Boston, incidentally. Did you know that?

S.L.   I know that. Hal Fenberg was writing with Harry, and socially he became aware of a character I did, a very Brooklyn-eze kind of character, who used malapropos. This preceded Norm Crosby.

Mel   Norm Crosby, yeah. Another Bostonian.

S.L.   Norm Crosby, he did malapropos. Like he would say that he was out taking the winter air in the Mojave Dessert [sic].

(Laughter)

S.L.   And, you know, mangle the language. What was it, yeah, broccacokali. Yeah, we used to eat broccacokali.

(Laughter)

S.L.   I used to do that kind of character for fun, and he asked if he could write it into the "Parkyakarkus" show, and I said, "Sure," and I did, and it was very well received, and the character became a permanent part of the show, a character called Orville Wright.

Mel   Oh, yes. Orville *Sharp*. Orville Sharp.

S.L.   No. Yes, Orville Sharp. You're quite right. Your memory is better than mine, and he would come on and say, "Am I correcked?" and do a spot based on malapropos. It became very popular.

And the other shows offered me variations on that kind of a thing. I then wound up, the next show that I did on a more regular basis was with Ann Sothern, the *Maisie* series.

Mel   Oh, that was great.

S.L.   From that followed Jack Benny and Phil —

Mel   Phil Harris?

S.L.   Phil Harris, and *Amos and Andy* and —

Mel   Judy Canova.

S.L.   Canova, all sorts of things, yes.

Mel   And, of course, one of my favorites, *The Damon Runyon Theatre*.

S.L.   Yeah. Well, that was in television.

Mel   No, no. Damon Runyon on radio.

S.L.   Oh, yeah, we did it on radio, but I thought you were referring to *The Damon Runyon Theatre*, which I put on television some years later.

Mel   Oh, I see. I see.

S.L.   I did a pilot based on the Damon Runyon [stories]. I don't remember that it was called *Damon Runyon Theatre*, but—

Mel   Yeah. It ran for one year on radio.

S.L.   Yes, indeed.

Mel   How about Jack Benny? The Benny show—which we all know and love you for—could you tell me how that started and developed for you?

S.L.   Well, again, it was a matter of a personal relationship. I did not exploit the characters I did for radio. I didn't go looking for jobs. The jobs by a set of circumstances came looking for me. For example, the character with Jack. The man who wrote that character was a man by the name of Milt Josefsberg.

Mel   Sure. I knew Milt.

S.L.   Well, Milt was my fishing companion. I used to go fishing with him down in Mexico periodically, and he proposed to design a character for me on *The Jack Benny Show*, and we talked about what kind of character it should be, and I said the things that seemed to be most acceptable from me were the semi-Runyonesque characters, the characters with a strong Brooklyn flavor, and with a kind of a dubious background, like a race-track tout, and Milt latched onto that, and he created a tout character, who was not, in fact, a race-track tout but who touted Jack off of things like what brand of chewing gum he was going to buy.

Mel   Sure.

S.L.   And everything but races.

Mel   From time to time you became involved with the commercials, Lucky Strike commercials. Do you recall any of those?

S.L.   Yes, I do. Yes, I do. That was a—the fact that I was always touting him off of one thing onto another was the basis of a very successful commercial, in which I said with my standard opening, "Hey, bud! Whatcha doin'?" and he'd say, "I'm going to the store." I'd say, "What for?" He said, "To buy some cigarettes." I'd say, "What brand?"

(Laughter)

S.L.   He'd say, "Lucky Strike," and now the audience is waiting for me to say, "Uh-uh," instead of which I'd say, "Hey, yeah, that's a very wise choice." So that commercial got a big play.

(Laughter)

Mel   How many years did you do Jack Benny on radio, Sheldon?

S.L.   About six.

Mel   And television as well?

S.L.   By the time he got into television I was already deeply involved in producing and directing television and had very little time, but whenever Jack requested my participation, I was very glad to do it and to push my program around so that I could do it. I did, oh, two or three or four appearances for him in the video version of his show.

Mel   I'd like to throw out some names to you, people that you were associated with throughout your radio career, and maybe in a few sentences if you could give us your opinion or reminiscences. Let's start with Judy Canova.

S.L.   Well, Judy Canova was a very nice lady, and the chemistry between us was good. She was not the hillbilly that she played, of course. She was quite a sophisticated lady and quite a generous lady, and I enjoyed working with her. I didn't get into her personal life to any degree, because she was a very private person, but I enjoyed the [professional] relationship with her.

Mel   How about Ann Sothern?

S.L.   Ann Sothern, well, she was also talented, but she—I don't know how to put it. She lived a very private life. She was at that time married to Bob Sterling, and they were not very approachable, not as with others where our professional life and social life sort of intermingled where we'd have dinners together and go on picnics together and things of that kind. Ann and Bob lived a very private life.

Mel   Phil Harris, Alice Faye?

S.L.   Oh, I was very fond of Phil, and we shared many activities together. He was an ardent fisherman as I was, and he loved to — he was devoted to golf as I was, and he liked the night out with the boys, as I did.

Mel   Nothing wrong with that. Freeman Gosden and Charles Correll?

S.L.   I know very little about them privately. Professionally, they were very adept. By the time I got to doing their show, they had been on the air for many years, and they had at one time been important enough in radio programming so that the traffic came to a halt when they were on the air, and toilets were flushed during the commercials, and all sorts of phenomena occurred related to their great popularity, but by the time I got with them they were getting a little long in the tooth and they were near the end of their career.

Mel   How about another great character actor, John Brown?

S.L.   Well, John did many of the kind of things that I did. He was more versatile than I am, but he did characters, and frequently I was credited with the characters he did. For example, he did a character with, oh, the big-bosomed lady. What was her name?

Mel   Marie Wilson?

S.L.   Marie Wilson.

Mel   *My Friend Irma*?

S.L.   Yeah. He did a character—

Mel   Oh, that's right. He was Al. He played Irma's boyfriend.

S.L.   That's right, and I was credited with that. Well, I had nothing to do with it, and typically he was frequently credited with some of the things that I did.

Mel   Sunday nights, you know, you did so many shows Sunday nights. Off the top of my head I'm thinking of Judy Canova, Phil Harris, Jack Benny, Amos and Andy.

S.L.   *Parkyakarkus* was also—

Mel   And *Parkyakarkus* was Sunday nights. I mean, you must have been one heck of a busy guy. How did you handle it all?

S.L.   Well, it wasn't that difficult. It was complicated, but not impossible. The way it worked was since we were doing the show on tape, we were not all competitive in terms of airtime. For example, I could do *The Jack Benny Show* at rehearsal at twelve o'clock, and do a two o'clock rehearsal on Judy Canova. There was an effort made to do the rehearsal and taping schedules in a time which accommodated the needs of the actors. I could very frequently do as many as three and four shows in a day.

Mel   Wow. And how far did you have to travel as far as the studios?

S.L.   Well, we have the distances between the—most of our work was at CBS and NBC. ABC didn't have a great deal for the little colony of radio actors that operated in Los Angeles at that time. Most of it was between CBS and NBC, and CBS and NBC were by a measured distance 350 yards apart.

Mel   Oh, wow. That's not bad.

S.L.   So you could go out of the back door of NBC and be entering onstage at CBS approximately 400 paces later, and approximately a minute and fifteen seconds later.

Mel   Tell us about your relationship with Jack Benny. What type of a guy was Jack Benny?

S.L.   The best. There were no better people either personally or professionally. Personally, of course, he was a generous and warm-hearted and friendly and approachable man. Professionally he was the epitome of professionalism, of professional integrity and of loyalty to his characters.

Mel   We've heard nothing but lovely things about Jack as a person. The characters on the Benny show, were they as close personally as they seemed on the air?

S.L.   Do you mean was Mel Blanc as much of a Mexican type as —

Mel   Well, no. No, no. No, I mean the camaraderie between all the actors on the show. Did they have a good relationship?

S.L.   To a degree. There was always a good relationship, but if I understand your use of the term camaraderie—no, we could not intermingle socially to too great an extent because, you know, *The Jack Benny Show* was only one element in our professional activities and we'd go from show to show, and we might choose—For example, I enjoyed a rewarding and enjoyable off-microphone relationship with Mel Blanc and with Elliot Lewis and with Hans Conried and with a few others, but then there were others who were part of that colony of actors that I had only a nodding acquaintance with.

Mel   What are your reminiscences of Elliot Lewis?

S.L   Elliot Lewis was about as brilliant in terms of intellectual capacity. He was very high on my list. As an actor, he was in the upper five percent, as far as I was concerned. As far as his professional career was concerned, as an actor, because he didn't—his appearance was not particularly glamorous, it was a little middle of the road appearance. He looked a little bit like a nice successful country insurance salesman, so his career as an actor was limited for that reason, but he then developed a very promising career as a director in radio, a producer and director in radio, and as a matter of fact, Elliot was responsible in a way, indirectly, for what my later career became, involved in television.

Mel   Which was producing and writing?

S.L.   Yes. You see the first things I sold, I sold to Elliot for the shows, the radio shows that he was directing, like *Broadway is My Beat*, and I can't remember the other names.

Mel   Oh, yeah.

S.L.   But I wrote half hour shows and Elliot bought them. Now, he bought seven or eight of them from me, and later when television was becoming a factor in our professional lives, I resold them. They reverted back to me after broadcast, and I resold them to—by adapting them for television, and as a result of selling that material to television I eventually began directing the material that I sold, and etcetera, etcetera, etcetera.

Mel   Let's talk a little bit about your terrific television career. You were associated with Danny Thomas for eleven years on TV as a—

S.L.   Yes. I produced and directed *The Danny Thomas Show.*

Mel   How did you become involved with that show?

S.L.   The William Morris Agency asked me if I would take a shot at it. When they put the show on the air, there were very few directors who had any comedy background, because television in the early fifties was a very poor medium that paid insignificant salaries, and the respected directors wouldn't touch it, but having no self-respect, I was approachable.

(Laughter)

S.L.   And I did have a comedy background that included Benny, Hope and etcetera, etcetera. But the Morris office in their search for a director who had some feeling for comedy, they fished—I at the time was doing pilots. I did the Damon Runyon pilot for *The Damon Runyon Theatre*. I did a pilot for a series called "The Jeweler's Showcase," and I had done two or three other pilots and was beginning to develop a reputation for having some aptitude for comedy, and the Morris office put me together with Danny.

Mel   What a show. Boy—eleven years.

S.L.   And off it we spun *The Andy Griffith Show*, and *The Andy Griffith Show* spun *The Gomer Pyle Show*, and while doing it I did *The Dick Van Dyke Show*…

Mel   Tell us a little bit about *The Dick Van Dyke Show*, Sheldon.

S.L.   Well, *The Dick Van Dyke Show* came about because Carl Reiner had made a pilot in New York called *Head of the Family*, which had not sold. They made it with Peter Lawford's money, and the thing had not sold, and he came—I was at that time running a thriving operation in situation comedy, and again, the Morris office asked if I would allow him to audit our operation so that he could get some sense for how successful situation comedies were put together, and I welcomed him, of course, and then learned that he had made this pilot for Lawford, and it had not sold, and I was very curious as to why that happened, because I recognized his talent as a writer. He did brilliant stuff, and I couldn't understand why it would not have sold.

Mel   In that pilot, didn't Morty Gunty play the Dick Van Dyke role, if I'm not mistaken?

S.L.   Not the Dick Van Dyke role—he played the Morey Amsterdam role.

Mel   Oh, the Morey Amsterdam role, and who played the Dick Van Dyke role?

S.L.   Carl Reiner.

Mel   *Carl Reiner?*

S.L.   And that's what was wrong with it.

Mel   Yes. Yes.

S.L.   That's why the pilot didn't sell. Carl was not right for it.

Mel   Yes.

S.L.   But when I read the material and saw it, I said, "Would you allow me to remake this with somebody else other than you?" and he was quite willing, and the one I chose to use was Van Dyke, and the rest is history.

Mel   What a great show. One of the all-time great TV shows.

S.L.   Well, it's still—You can see it every night on *Nick at Nite*.

Mel   Tell me, I was curious, you've done so many movies, and in a sense we all have a tendency to pluck at a given picture for one reason or another and ask about people you've known. I was curious about whether you ever really got to know Cesar Romero from one of your pictures back in the forties.

S.L.   I know Cesar Romero quite well. He did one of my first—my second picture in Hollywood. The first picture was a *Thin Man* picture. The second one was a thing at Twentieth Century Fox called *Tall, Dark and Handsome*.

Mel.   Which is the film I was thinking of.

S.L.   And I worked in it with Cesar Romero, who we called Butch, and Butch and I are contemporaries. A few people realize that Butch has been around as long as he has, but Butch and I were graduates from the Broadway theatre in the thirties, and I'm eighty-six and Butch is eighty-five.

Mel.   And I've noticed whenever I've seen Cesar in anything, and he has been making appearances and things, he looks like he's in very good shape.

S.L.   He's in great shape, and he's one of the most attractive men in Hollywood and one of the most in demand as an escort, and I'm very fond of him. He's a very nice man.

Mel.   Now, one aspect of—you've kind of segued into television here—which is inevitable—movies, shows and radio, and probably your greatest success has really been in television. The one show that was not mentioned was *I Spy*, which was not only a landmark series for the sixties, but I understand it's going to be done for the first time as a renewed production sometime in the fall. I wonder what your involvement with that was in the reuniting of Bill Cosby and Robert Culp.

S.L.   Well, my involvement is that I am creating it, I am doing it. I'm responsible for it.

Mel.   That's great to hear.

Mel   Of all the things that you've done, what would you say is your favorite?
        Did you enjoy acting, or radio—

S.L   I enjoy putting together the elements of a show and guiding it into a
        career. I enjoy putting together *Van Dyke*, *Andy Griffith*, *Gomer Pyle*, *I
        Spy*. That's fun. I like that.

Mel   Yeah, that's good. I've heard this, and I wonder if you could corrobo-
        rate this for me. Nickelodeon has said a couple of times that the net-
        work was going to cancel Dick Van Dyke-

S.L.   They did, at the end of the first year, they made a cancellation of it.

Mel   And you went up and talked them into continuing with it.

S.L.   I went to Cincinnati. The sponsor was Procter & Gamble, and I
        persuaded them to revoke the cancellation.

Mel   That's amazing. It's a good thing you did. I hope they were happy.
        Well, I promised I'd have you off for your dinner hour, Sheldon.

S.L.   Which is now.

Mel   What's for dinner? I might be over!

S.L.   Anytime, Mel. Goodnight.

Steve Allen

STEVE VALENTINE PATRICK WILLIAM ALLEN (DECEMBER 26, 1921-OCTO-
BER 30, 2000) was an actor, comedian, composer, musician, writer and media
personality. Steve's mother was a vaudeville comic and Steve—as the saying
goes—"grew up in a trunk." Milton Berle often babysat for the youngster when
Steve's mother was onstage. Although he got his start in radio, he is best
remembered for his television work. In 1954 he became the first host of *The
Tonight Show*, and during his three-year reign innovated the concept of the
television talk show. Steve Allen was an erudite, accomplished individual, with
some fifty books and several hundred songs to his name. He had many other
credits as well, and he discussed these for me during a lengthy telephone conversation on February 27, 1997. It is one of my favorite interviews ...

S.A.   Hello?

Mel   Steve?

S.A.   Who's calling?

Mel   This is Mel Simons calling from Boston.

S.A.   Oh, hi, Mel. How are you?

Mel   I'm fine. How are you?

S.A.   A little punchy. I just got off an airplane from Aspen, Colorado.

Mel   Yes. Your secretary was telling me.

S.A.   I'm at your service.

Mel   I thank you very, very much, Steve.

S.A.   Okay.

Mel   I'd like to begin by asking you a few questions, Steve.

S.A.   All right. Mel, if I may interrupt you for one moment. Roughly how long will we be involved?

Mel   Approximately 45 minutes, if that's okay with you.

S.A.   Okay. I therefore have to give somebody here a message. I'll be with you in about three seconds.

Mel   Okay. Fine.

(Pause)

S.A.   Okay, go ahead.

Mel   All right. Steve, I'd like to begin with your mom and dad. I know
          your mom and dad were a comedy team in vaudeville.

S.A.   Correct.

Mel   Your mom was the comedian and your dad was the straight man.

S.A.   That's right, and he also sang. Yeah, that was their relationship.

Mel   And I had the pleasure of meeting Milton Berle not too long ago, and
          one of the things I got a kick out of was Milton Berle telling me that he
          babysat for you.

S.A.   That is true. Probably only two or three times, but he was on the bill
          with my mother. How many times that occurred I don't know, but a
          few times. He was probably twelve or fourteen at the time. He was in
          vaudeville then, as you know.

Mel   So you actually got your start growing up as a youngster watching
          mom and dad perform.

S.A.   Yes. I don't have much in the way of conscious recollection of my father,
          but simply because he died when I was a year and a half old, but I clearly
          remember seeing my mother on stage many instances. She worked with a
          number of partners after my father's death, and Milton, who as I say worked
          with her, was once kind enough to refer to her as the funniest woman in
          vaudeville, or something to that effect, and I believe she was.

Mel   When did you lose your mom, Steve.

S.A.   Seems to be she's been gone for about fifteen years or so.

Mel   Were you bitten by, well, the show-biz bug as a youngster?

S.A.   No, I had no conscious interest in it at all to the extent that I was
          aiming at anything, and it was a career in journalism. I had discovered

early the ability to write and speak coherently. I didn't think that was a gift. I just thought that's what everybody was supposed to be able to do. It was only some years later that I realized not many can.

Mel   And you attended Arizona State Teacher's College.

S.A.   I attended eighteen schools in all, of which that was one, yes.

Mel   Eighteen schools!

S.A.   Yes. I didn't plan it that way. I would not advise others to do the same but that's what happened.

Mel   Off the top of your head, Steve, could you name a few of the schools that you attended?

S.A.   Well, most of them would mean nothing to you. To state from the top, the last one I did attend, and only for about four months of my sophomore year, was Arizona State. It's now the famous football university. At that time it only had a student body of about 1,500 people.

Then the year before that on a journalism scholarship I attended Drake University in Des Moines, Iowa, and it was there that I sort of got sidetracked so that I ended up in radio.

Mel   Tell us about that.

S.A.   Well, it's a good school. At the time I went there it had a very good radio production course, and I honestly took it simply because it seemed like a snap course as compared to studying German or chemistry or something that would require some real work.

I had already discovered in myself the ability, as I mentioned earlier, to communicate. My mother's family had the, to use that old expression, the gift of gab, and I had tried real work in a couple of instances and didn't enjoy it too much, so I thought for a avidly lazy person such as myself, radio might make a great deal of sense.

In any event, as I say, that's how I got off the track and ended up in radio.

Mel   Tell us about your first job in radio, Steve.

S.A.   Well, the first regular job, real job, was at a CBS station in Phoenix called KOY. This was around 1943, I guess, and I worked there for three years and took about six months off in the Army at one point, but they were three wonderful years. If I had had the money I would have paid them for the experience, because after I was hired, which was just to be an announcer, certainly the world's easiest work, then they discovered that I had a number of other abilities, and they immediately called all of them into play, so that within a few months I was writing the majority of the commercial copy for the station and writing news and reading news and producing news.

Mel   Disc jockey work as well?

S.A.   Not very much of that. The term *disc jockey* hadn't even been invented in those days. If you were an announcer and if your station played some records, then that would be simply one of various things you might do. You'd do commercials. You'd do news, and in those days, if you were lucky enough to work at a network station, which KOY was, you would be called upon to do quite a few things, so of all those things, playing records was the least important thing.

Mel   So that was really your basic training in show biz.

S.A.   Yes. That has nothing much to do with my other work in lounges as a piano player and singer and my work starting around that time doing standup comedy, but it did keep the paychecks coming in, and it was a delightful learning experience.

Mel   Did you start playing piano as a youngster?

S.A.   Yes, I took sort of typical school or neighborhood lessons starting, I guess, when I was about eight or so, but nothing much "took" because we had no piano at home, so the lessons added up to nothing much. If you can't practice whatever you learned in a lesson, you forget in three or four days, so I just played around with it a little just as if it was a hobby like table tennis or anything else, but then in my teenage years starting at about thirteen or fourteen, I became more seriously interested, and as often happens with people in the creative arts, there were successful role models. You know, a young actor might want to grow up to be another James Dean or Marlon Brando or Donald Duck or whoever, so one of the most popular people in the music industry in those days was a pianist named Eddie Duchin.

Mel   Oh, sure. From this area, from Boston.

S.A.   That's right, and they eventually made a motion picture of his life starring Tyrone Power, so every young American boy in those days who had any ability to play the piano, even if you didn't play very well, had these James Thurber*ish* daydreams of growing up to be an Eddie Duchin. So, on the basis of that little inspiration, I began to pick up little chords here and there and things from different friends of mine who knew a little about the instrument, and I gradually taught myself to play by ear, and that's worked out well since.

Mel   Now, when did the standup comedy start? How did that begin?

S.A.   Well, that began actually in high school, because in this particular case it was a Hyde Park High School in Chicago where Mel Torme was a student at the same time, and I was always—and this is true of the lives of most people who end up as professional comics—I was always a bit of the neighborhood cutup or the class clown—that sort of thing.

         So some sweet young girls came to me on day and said, "We think you're funny, and we're going to have a special show," and they mentioned some date coming up, a week or two down the line, in the afternoon, just a thing in a classroom. "Would you come and do something for us?" To that point I'd never done anything that I'd looked upon as entertainment. You know, I just got laughs in the playground or at the drugstore. So I said, "Sure," as if I had an act. I had nothing.

         So what I actually ended up doing, since it never occurred to me that I could get away in front of an audience doing the kind of silly talk that I did among my friends, I actually read aloud and gave it property attribution, a classic reading by my then idol, an American humorist named Robert Benchley.

Mel   Sure.

S.A.   And it was called "The Treasurer's Report." It's still recognized as something of a classic.

Mel   Yes.

S.A.   So, you know, that's not too funny—I mean, not too *difficult*. But I realized it wasn't *my* material, so after that I did my own things, but that was the first step.

Mel   Now, after the Army as far as your radio work, did KNX come next in Los Angeles?

S.A.   Yeah, that's correct. In those days, as I'm sure you know, because of your historical interest, the people who worked in radio, who were not simply content to stay in Wilkes Barre or East Overshoe, Idaho, or wherever they were working, and many of them were, and there's nothing wrong with that, but those who had somewhat greater ambitions headed for three major targets.

If you were in the East you wanted to end up in New York. If you were in the Midwest, Chicago was your destination of choice, and on the West Coast it was Los Angeles. For obvious reasons they were big radio capitals in those days, so since I was already in the West, Los Angeles was what I had in mind, and I worked, as I say, for about three years or so in Phoenix and saved money.

I actually didn't make much more than enough to live on at the radio station, but at nights for quite a long time I was playing the piano and singing in a restaurant that I believe still exists there called The Steak House. They had a dining room and a little room with a piano and a bar and so forth. So it was there I was able to put all The Steak House money aside as a sort of a travel fund and finally was able to make the jump over to Los Angeles.

To return to your earlier question about comedy, there was a fellow announcer on the staff, a fellow named Wendall Noble. He's gone now. And he had a cute sense of humor, and the two of us used to horse around together, so we finally put an act together. I played the piano; he sang. He had a nice sort of a legitimate Nelson Eddy-type singing voice, and we did a little, cute little humorous touches and silly songs together, and it doesn't take that much to put together, you know, a fifteen- or twenty-minute act so . So we had an act of sorts, he preceded me in Los Angeles, so when I got there, I looked him up, and then we began to do some dates in and around town.

So that was another step in the comedy direction.

Mel   Last night I was listening to your recording on KNX where you interviewed Al Jolson.

S.A.   Yeah. That's quite a memorable night.

Mel   You took the words right out of my mouth, Steve. I mean, it floored me. It was just sensational. Your rapport with Jolson. What are your personal memories, and what was the year? Around '49 or '50?

S.A.   Gosh, I'd forgotten that. Well, what I didn't know until years later was that a lot of the Hollywood crème de la crème used to listen to the show every night. Ethel Barrymore, Fannie Brice, people to me—those were names that were like the names of Thomas Jefferson or Abe Lincoln.

Mel   Sure.

S.A.   And Katharine Hepburn used to listen to the show every night and quite a few others I'll probably think of later. One day I opened my modest fan mail, I think I got about eight letters a day at their peak, and one of them was a lovely three-page letter handwritten from a comedian whose work I had great respect for and who later would meet—Phil Silvers.

      Parenthetically, I learned something from that, because I knew that I was so impressed as a young unknown to get a letter from such an Olympian figure. Since then over the years I've written many such letters myself to people I thought deserved to be praised and encourage, but yeah, that show became an institution very quickly. Not so much because it was the greatest show of all time but because there was nothing else like it. Everything else was news or, I don't know, you know, repeats of soap operas or God knows what they had on the air. Mostly it was just playing records by that time.

Mel   How long was the show?

S.A.   You mean, per night it ran?

Mel   Per night, yeah.

S.A.   I think it was a sixty-minute show. It started as a thirty-minute show, and then because it caught on they lengthened it to sixty, and it was at that point I began interviewing people, because before that I had done more or less conventional radio comedy—conventional in form. At first you wrote it, and then you stood in front of a microphone and read your script the way both the great shows and the terrible shows were done. They're all done with scripts in hand, but since they gave me no more money when they increased the show to sixty minutes, I thought, *I'll be damned if I'm gonna spend more time at the typewriter.*

      So I just took the easy way out and began to interview people, and then came an important accident.

      It's remarkable over the course of my career how many things just sort of fell off the tree, because of a mistake or something negative that turned into a positive, but one night my scheduled guest was Doris Day. She was at the peak of her film career at that time, and always a wonderful singer. So to get to the point, Doris didn't show up. It later turned out somebody had forgotten to tell her that she was supposed to, but there I was on the air live with 30 minutes to fill, and not a thought in my head, so acting on automatic pilot I just — I had never gone into an audience before. I picked up the old standup microphone, the old cheese box type, as they used to call it, and carried this heavy piece of equipment up and down the aisle of the theatre and got bigger laughs doing that than I'd ever gotten with scripted material, even though that had worked out well, too.

It suddenly occurs to me I left a two-year blank here in that to refer back to Wendall Noble, my comedy partner, in 1946 and '47, he and I for two years did our own daily comedy show on the Mutual Radio Network.

Mel   Out of L.A.?

S.A.   Yeah, in Hollywood. So anyway, there was that background, and that sort of propelled me into the late night thing for CBS.

Mel   Now, this was again kind of your basic training as far as hosting *The Tonight Show*. Can you tell us how that developed?

S.A.   Exactly. Well, the three-year stretch of that late-night radio show gave me a chance to do everything with the ability that I found within myself, to play the piano, to sing, and to horse around, and to speak without script, and that comes in handy if you're a talk-show host. Not all talk-show hosts work that way. In fact, there are two totally separate forms of talk-shows. One is *The Tonight Show* type where it helps if you have some ability to get laughs yourself, and then there's the other type that we used to call the theme show. They were both created during my tenure in office, so to speak.

        Some nights we would just discuss organized crime or narcotics addiction or some important social issue, and that would be our theme for the night, and we wouldn't go for comedy on those nights.

Mel   Oh, it really was serious?

S.A.   Oh, yeah, on certain nights, and even when—to jump now to *The Tonight Show*, that was a talk show most nights but not every night. I've never enjoyed narrowing myself into a small formula partly because I can't control the ability to adlib anyway, and that's easier to do if there's latitude, you know, if the boundaries are loose.

But one of the great nights of *The Tonight Show* came when our one guest for the ninety minutes was Richard Rodgers, the great composer, and the show was so simple; it was hardly produced. We sat Mr. Rodgers down at the piano and we had all four of our wonderful singers there that night: Steve Lawrence, Eydie Gormé, Andy Williams and a woman named Pat Kirby, and then every so often Mr. Rodgers would say to me, "You play this one. I heard you do it the other night," or whatever, "I've heard your recording of it." So I would spend a little time at the piano, he would jump in, and it was hardly rehearsed at all.

We had sheet music right there on the piano, and it was ninety minutes of the best television ever, but obviously that night it was not a talk show.

Mel   Wow. What years did you do *The Tonight Show?*

S.A.   Well, it started as a local show in New York, just called *The Steve Allen Show,* because the shows were the names of the people who headed them up, and then like the earlier radio example, it caught on, because there was nothing else like it on television, so the NBC people came to me and said, "We like your show, and we'd like to put it on the whole network at night." So I said, "Okay."

And at that point they changed the name of it from *The Steve Allen Show* to *Tonight,* because Pat Weaver, who was running the network in those days had an already successful experiment on in the morning called *Today,* which is still with us. Dave Garroway was the first host, I believe, so he obviously wanted something late at night called *Tonight,* and he just chose my program and put that new name on it.

Mel   And what year are we talking now, Steve?

S.A.   Well, it started as I say locally in 1953, and it went on I recall about fourteen months later, so some time in, I think it was, the fall of 1954 it hit the network, and then I did it for the next, I think it was, four years or three. I forget.

Anyway, I was there for a total of four years.

Mel   Now, if memory serves me right, weren't you at the beginning also doing your Sunday night show the same time as you were doing *The Tonight Show?*

S.A.   Well, not at the beginning, no. But what happened was—the network had a very serious problem. I have no interest in their problems. I was busy doing my own things, but the problem was, what the heck to do about *The Ed Sullivan Show*, which had already been on the air, I don't know, let's say, ten years and was a national institution. Everybody liked to watch Ed and the vaudeville acts every Sunday night, and NBC had put some very formidable affair in opposite him. People like Dean Martin and Jerry Lewis and guests like Frank Sinatra and Jimmy Durante. They threw some big names at him.

Mel   Oh, *The Colgate Comedy Hour.*

S.A.   *The Colgate Comedy Hour*, yes, and none of them could put much of a dent in Ed's ratings, so I still don't know how many other possibilities they had in mind, but they came to me next, because *The Tonight Show* had quickly become a hit, and they thought I might have the same good luck there, and I was so young then and enjoyed working so much. I'm no longer so young, but I still enjoy working, so I said, "Yeah. Sure. Fine." And I quickly realized after I, for a while, did both shows that I had something of a problem.

There was no problem with *The Tonight Show.* I think hosting a talk show is a very easy assignment. The guests have to be talented, but you don't, you know, if all you do is interview people and say, "Now, here he is, Bing Crosby!" and Bing has to be great, but all you have to say is "Here he is." It's like the Jolson show, you know. But that as I say was not the problem, but the other show was a major, big budget, prime-time production, and to this day I think the two best sketch comedy shows of that sort I would rate the Sid Caesar program as No. 1, and our own show No. 2, because we too had a wonderful comedy company. I'm talking about people like Don Knots and Louis Nye and Bill Dana.

Mel   Wonderful cast of characters, Second Bananas.

S.A.   They were great, yes.

Mel   How did they all develop, all these characters, and how did they get started with you?

S.A.   Well, it was a different story in each case. At the time I was starting in '53 with that particular series, there was on an ABC station in New York a late night show, a variety show, a lot of music, and it was judged as, other than having some good singers, it was really an awful show. Very disorganized, and they had about four hosts, which never makes any sense, and none of them were really qualified. One was a radio fellow, and then somebody else was a singer. It was just a dumb, loose show.

But in this morass of lightweight stuff there was one fellow who invariably made me laugh whenever I saw him, and I'd never heard of him. His name was Louis Nye. Didn't matter what he did, he was just funny. That's very often the way that you can distinguish the superior comedians from just another funny fellow. The other funny fellows generally have to have good strong material or big strong jokes to make you laugh, but the really funny people like Jonathan Winters or Robin Williams, Donald Duck, whoever you laugh at, they're just funny when they show up and the material is a second matter.

(Laughter)

S.A.   So he struck me that way, and I had met him by chance in the RCA building one day, and I said, "Oh, are you that guy on that late night show?" I said, "Listen, NBC is talking to me about starting a program of my own, and if you have no other plans, I'd like you to jump in from time to time." He said, "Okay."

So sure enough, the show happened, and I called him, and that's how he joined us.

Then in the case of Don Knotts, now, we're jumping to about 1956 or so. Even then, I did what all talk-show hosts do: you book other comics and have them do stand-up routines that they all have perfected, so Don did two standup routines that were literally classics—almost in the Robert Benchley tradition—just little gems, so he had the good fortune to come to my attention just about the time I was going on the full network in prime time, so that's how he joined us.

In the case of Tom Poston—who was really more of a comedy actor than a comedian in the sense that Bob Hope is a comedian—he just began to hang around the production office.

We had no security guards. Almost anybody could walk in—

Mel   Wow.

S.A.   —and hang out. Today you'd have to get through all kinds of policemen.

Mel   Yeah, I would think so.

S.A.   But we ran a big open sort of a fraternity house atmosphere, and he was around for weeks before we ever figured out a way to put him on the air, and then the writers developed this character, the guy who was so stupid, he can't even remember his own name. We put him into the "Man in the Street" routines.

Mel   One of my favorites was Bill Dana.

S.A.   Oh, yeah.

Mel   Incidentally from this town that we're calling you from.

S.A.   Oh, that's right.

Mel   From Quincy, Wollaston area. How did Bill start with you?

S.A.   Well, he started as a writer. I don't remember who it was that recommended him, but it's interesting today when a show of that general sort wins an award, it almost looks like a comedy routine itself. Forty-eight people get up out of the audience to get their statues. You'll never guess how many writers I had when the late night show started, so I'll save you some time. The answer was none at all.

Mel   Wow.

S.A.   When we were having the preplanning business meetings to make out a budget, they said, "Do you need any writers?" I said, "To write what? I adlib." They said, "Okay. Forget that." So I finally did get writers in and some wonderful ones, but there were none when we started, so Bill was in there early. I don't remember the exact year, and he was funny around the office. He did funny dialects, and I wanted him to do some things on the air, so he finally worked out this Latino character for himself called José Jiménez, and it was funny them. Still *is* funny.

Mel   It certainly is. I remember some of your guests so well, in fact, I'd like to throw out a few names at you, Steve, and just have you comment. I can remember Lou Costello guesting on your show. Not Abbott—just Lou Costello.

S.A.   Yeah. After Abbott and Costello went their separate ways—we had had them on as a team before that, but after that we booked Lou for seems to me six or seven different appearances, and in most cases he did sketches that he had done before in vaudeville or burlesque or new material it might have been. So he was always great fun to work with.

Mel   How about Bing Crosby?

S.A.   This is really a stupid response. Knowing about Bing Crosby, at least if you're of my generation, it's like knowing Santa Claus or Thomas Jefferson. Somebody that dominant in the American culture, we all sort of felt we knew him, and I did meet Bing a couple of times over the years, but I honestly can't recall if he was ever my guest. I told you it would sound stupid, but I can't.

He was kind enough to record one of my songs, so he was very important in my career as a songwriter quite earlier. I had written the lyric to a Dixieland classic called "The South Rampart Street Parade."

Mel   Oh, sure.

S.A.   Which parenthetically went over very well last week, because I just came back from doing four shows in New Orleans, but when he and the Andrews Sisters recorded that, that saved me about ten years of knocking on doors as a songwriter, because he and the Andrews Sisters were then about the No. 1 singers in the business.

Mel   I can also remember Elvis Presley on your show.

S.A.   Oh, yeah.

Mel   What are your memories of him?

S.A.   Well, sometimes I'm credited with discovering Elvis, but that's not a correct assessment, because that implies I found him in the Met Market and said, "Hey, kid, you ought to get into show business." I found him on television. In other words, he did not start on my show. I had him before Ed Sullivan did, but that's a separate question, too.

So I was watching television at random one night, and Jackie Gleason, who always good big bands and good music generally had a summer replacement—

Mel   Oh, the Dorseys. Yeah.

S.A.   Yeah. Jimmy and Tommy Dorsey, the saxophone and trombone players, and since I shared Gleason's taste in music, I just happened to be watching that show one night, and [there was] this kind of goofy, gangly kid, totally unknown to me at that point. I didn't even catch his name that night. But—not to coin a phrase—*he had something.* There was something, star quality, some mystery thing nobody can ever describe what it was that James Dean had or Marilyn Monroe or Elvis or Clark Gable. There are just some people that something magical happens when they go on stage or on the screen. So I recognized that in him immediately, and so I just wrote a little hand note, and then the following morning at the office I said, "Find out who that kid was last night on the Dorsey show, and let's have him as a guest on this new thing." This was when I was starting the prime time comedy show.

So then we just had a bit of good luck. He was totally unknown to America that night that I saw him, but there were about six weeks that passed between that moment and when he finally appeared, and suddenly, thanks oddly enough to so much criticism of him by Ed Sullivan, who said he would never book anybody so vulgar and—

Mel   Oh, it was something about shooting below the waist, his gyrating.

S.A.   Yeah. It was all so stupid. Anyway, Ed was responsible for making Elvis so big by his putting him down that we got a free ride the night he showed up, and the rating was so big that Sullivan panicked, because he had been invulnerable until our show showed up, and here on our second night we got the higher rating, so he called Colonel Parker backstage at our theatre that very night, believe it or not, and immediately made the booking. We wouldn't have known it, except apparently he made his first call during the show, and then after we were off the air, our producer, Billy Harbeck, came to me and he said, "I'm talking to the Colonel here, and he says that Ed called him a few minutes ago," and he said, "Here's the situation."

As you may recall, in those days, the top price no matter who you were was $7,500. That's a hell of a lot of money to find on the sidewalk. It would be, oh, like $20,000 today, I guess. So nobody got more than that. There was no negotiation.

But in this case Sullivan's desperation made him break that price ceiling, and moreover, he offered Elvis five appearances, a guarantee of five appearances.

There must be a lot of young people listening who don't even know who Ed Sullivan is. Some who don't know who I am, for that matter, but I should explain that Ed was never an entertainer. In fact, he was so inept as a speaker that all the comedians made fun of him, and that helped also to make him more lovable and more endearing, because it seemed to people, *Hey, he's one of us. He's not even clever, but we love his show.*

So anyway, he was always a journalist, which was his trade. He was a newspaper man. He knew what was news. He knew what was hot, and—could you hang on for just one second?

Mel   Absolutely.

S.A.   There's an emergency here.

Mel   Surely. Go right ahead, Steve.

(Pause)

S.A   Yeah.

Mel   Okay.

S.A.   I now realize it wasn't an emergency. Jayne [Meadows, Steve's wife] is doing some work here in the kitchen as we talk, Mel, and she just reminded me she was in those days for seven years, in fact, on the panel of the old *I've Got A Secret.*

Mel   Of course, *The Garry Moore Show.*

S.A.   Yes. And she was just reminding me of something that Garry said at that point. He said, "Steve will do the better show, but he will never beat Sullivan in the ratings, because Steve will book people on the basis of their talent, and Ed will book people on the basis of their news value that week." Whoever, you know, threw the pass that won the Rose Bowl Game or whatever it was or whoever, you know, Muhammad Ali knocked somebody down, whatever the big news, those were his booking guidelines, so he knew that Elvis was hot stuff in terms of popular interest, and he was right about that.

Mel   Was there ever a conflict problem? Did you ever have a problem booking a guest because Sullivan had used him?

S.A.   Well, there was a competitive situation, yes. I hated that part of it, because I'm an entertainer. I'm not a lawyer or a—that whole aspect of show business always had a negative effect on me, but it was a reality and we did have to fact it.

I never knew that much about it, because even though there were certain times we could not get a particular guest, at first you might think, *Oh, isn't that terrible.* Well the answer is, it wasn't so terrible, because we had 419 people we could book, so I never cared who we had or when we had them, you know, as long as they were good. I was glad to get them when I could.

But there was actually a federal investigation, which I found out about when a man from the—I forgot which branch of the federal government set up an appointment with me, and apparently somebody had sued, I don't know who it was, one of the major agencies, which happened to handle Ed Sullivan, for throwing their best guests his way, and apparently that was considered restraint of trade or malfeasance in office or whatever the heck it was considered.

So, yeah, there was that problem, and also, Ed was not above throwing his weight around, and there were occasional reports of agents would say "Hey, I'd rather put my client on your show, because you have more fun and yours is a comedy show, not a variety show, but what can I do? Sullivan threatens that if I do that, you know, we'd better not bother him about bookings in the future." So he did use his muscle in that way.

Mel   This is kind of a general question, Steve. But looking back on your Sunday night show, some of your personal favorite guests. If you could pick say a top five or six that you really, really loved, who would they be?

S.A.   Gosh, that's a marvelous question, and I don't know if I can come up with an equally marvelous answer. I love talent. I've always loved talent, and we really did as Garry Moore predicated. We did go for that factor, and in some cases that meant looking for big people like a Sinatra or whoever, but in many cases it also meant booking an unknown, who just happened to sing great or play the trumpet great or whatever they did, so there's no little group of names that comes to mind.

Among my favorites, of course, was Peter Ustinov, the English entertainer and playwright and bon vivant, a very entertaining fellow. I was with him last year in Chicago, and we had a marvelous time together, so his name does pop up in that connection, and other than that there was sort of all of the above. I don't have any particular names that we kept going back to.

Mel   How many years did you do the Sunday night show?

S.A.   That was on for four years, and then the fifth season I went over and did the show in 1961 on ABC.

Mel   And I think did you change nights—Monday night?

S.A.   Yeah. NBC originally had this on Sunday nights. We were there for years, and then I think they moved us to a Wednesday, and then I think to a Monday.

Mel   See, if I recall, I think it was Monday. That's the first time I ever saw Jackie Mason perform.

S.A.   Yes. I introduced Jackie to TV, and he was wonderfully funny as always.

Mel   And I'll show you how vivid my memory is, Steve. I was so impressed with him, you had him on one night, and then two weeks later you brought him back.

S.A.   Umm-hmm. Yeah. You remember things I don't.

Mel   You wrote four thousand songs the last time I looked and about fifty books.

S.A.   Well, the books now, forty-eight have been published, and three more are coming out in the next year, so the number of songs is now up to over 6,300, yeah.

Mel   When I watched you on the show, one of my favorite bits that you often did was the reading of the lyrics of the up and coming rock 'n' roll songs.

S.A.   Right. I still do that routine. I do the songs, yeah. In fact, I still remember the popular song that I started with. It was a big No. 1 hit then called "Love Somebody."

> Yes, I do
> Love somebody
> Yes, I do
> Love somebody
> Yes, I do/Love somebody
> But I won't say who

(Laughter)

Mel   What was Dayton Allen like?

S.A.   A very clever actor, and he was and still is to this day the definitive comic Dracula [Bela Lugosi]. In fact, all of the other comedians, who since his time have done Dracula are basically doing his version of Dracula.

I once described Dayton Allen as the Jewish Jonathan Winters. He's got that same free form, anything for a laugh, a million ideas a minute. One of the funniest men you will ever meet. So funny, in fact, that it's very difficult to have a sensible conversation with him. I never have had one. Every time we talk to each other, whether on the phone or in person, it's craziness, but that's the way his mind works, and as funny as he was on the air, and he was always terrific, he was even funnier just hanging around.

He also had in common with Jonathan that they could never [turn it off]. Jayne and I were on a cruise with Jonathan several years back, and on those cruises it's nice duty. You do your show in the evening, and maybe if it's a big ship, you do two shows and that's it. For the next several days you have nothing to do.

Well, Jonathan was part of the same touring group, and if I got up at three in the morning and went downstairs just to get some fresh air, I would find him entertaining two people in the lounge.

Mel   Wow.

S.A.   One guy leaning against the rail. He would still be talking like mad.

(Laughter)

S.A.   So Dayton had that same crazy quality, but very funny.

Mel   I wanted to ask you. I've always been a big fan of Fred Allen. The parallels between Fred Allen's *Allen's Alley* and your Man in the Street, I'm wondering to what extent Fred Allen influenced you.

S.A   Well, I always loved Fred Allen. First of all, I loved him personally. We were good friends, and he was one of my favorite comedians, because even when I was sixteen, what did I know? I could see he was a witty man, and he wrote a good deal, if not all, of his own material, and his material always had a definite stamp to it. It was not just—you couldn't have written earlier for Bob Hope or Red Skelton and then automatically move into writing for Fred Allen. It was a different order of humor.

One of the reasons that I always loved his jokes, his material, was there was a kind of a strange poetic Irish element to some of his routines.

For example, one of them, just a joke, was a story about a—not a story, just a line, about a scarecrow ... Everybody knows what a scarecrow is; it stands in a cornfield. Well, he said, this particular scarecrow was so scary that it not only scared the crows away, but they were so scared they brought back corn that they had stolen two years earlier.

(Laughter)

S.A.   I love that kind of a joke, and that was typical of his humor.

Mel   He was wonderful.

S.A.   However, as regards the similarity between our shows, I don't believe there was any. There was *Allen's Alley*, of course, which was marvelous, but my Man on the Street routine was simply making fun of what had been, I guess, for about two hundred years a staple of journalism, and you see it in papers all over the—I saw *USA Today*, and they have it every day. There's a question of the day: Should Hillary Clinton stay there, or whatever the question might be and they send out a photographer and a reporter, and they put the question to four or five people, and they run their answers. You'll find that in most of the world's newspaper letters to the editor.

No. Those are two totally separate routines. When I first got to New York, although I was born there, I never lived there, but all during the fifties I was there doing TV, and when I first got there in my capacity as a newcomer to town, a tourist, so to speak, with a fresh eye, I noticed that the letters of complaint that were published chiefly in *The New York Daily* were the angriest, most vituperative, abusive, insulting letters I'd ever read, and something about their extreme exaggerations struck me funny, so I didn't say, *Ah, here's a routine I'll do for the next twenty years.* I just tried it one night, and it got such screams.

I would say to the audience, "Did you see today's news?" whatever, whether you did or not, I don't care. Some people wrote these letters, and they're all real letters, and the people are furious, and I said, "But very often when you read them, maybe for you it's a nice day. Maybe the weather's good. Maybe your wife just kissed you on the mouth," whatever happened in your life, it's pleasant, and therefore, you don't really care that these people are screaming about too many pigeons in the park in New York, or whatever, you know, Communists or whatever turns them on, and I said, "I don't think that's right. If you were burned up about something, you'd want others to share your reaction, wouldn't you?" And at this point the band and the crowd would start to say, "Yeah, damn right," and so forth, so I would say, "Well, I'm going to read these letters," and then I would read the letters without changing a word but for a little protective finish. Instead of using the word or the actual sender, I would lift that out and put in some name that made it automatically a joke. For example, if there was a real letter that said something like, "We've got to do something with the degree of alcoholism in our society. It is sickening. It is destroying the fiber of American society," *blah, blah, blah*, and then I would say, "Signed, Dean Martin."

(Laughter)

S.A.   Whatever the joke was, and that was just a little bit of protection so you'd be sure you got a laugh at the finish. But that's how that started, and over the years, all of the letters were real. We never had to write a single—in fact, it would have ruined it if we made up those letters.

Mel   And where did the catch phrase "How's your bird?" come from?

S.A.   Well, one of my dear friends during my years in New York was a very funny comedian. He was only on TV now and then, so he never got that well known, but a very witty man and a lovely fellow named Fat Jack Leonard or Jack E. Leonard.

Mel   Oh, Jack E. Leonard, sure.

S.A.   He's been described as the original Don Rickles in that he worked with the kind of brusque, insulting manner.

Mel   You starred in the movie *The Benny Goodman Story*.

S.A.   Yes.

Mel   What I wondered about was, did Goodman basically approve of the Hollywood treatment, or did he feel that things like that incredible way that Fletcher Henderson was supposed to have listened and glided into a cab—?

S.A.   Well, Benny did have approval of the script. We know that. I never asked him, but that's par for the course. If they do your life, you have something to say about what the script says, and the story was in large strokes substantially true, but, of course, Terry Gibbs, the great jazz player, worked with me, and after he saw the movie he said, "The thing

I didn't like, " he said, "you made Benny seem like a lover." And he said, "He was never a lover." He must have loved Alice, and they did get married, but anyway, I was playing myself, because nobody knew. To this day people don't know anything about Benny except his marvelous playing. Still the greatest clarinet jazz player of them all.

Mel   But a very private man.

S.A.   Very private man, and now that he's gone, we can speak frankly, a very dull man.

(Laughter)

S.A.   I said to the director and producer, I said, "We all know Benny." I said, "Do you really want me to be like him? Do you want me to be at all cute or funny?" They said, No. We're taking a risk hiring a comedian to do this, because some people have already mentioned what sense does that make?" They said, "So just stick with the script," and so that's what I did. Nobody knew what he spoke like, so I didn't have to do him in the sense that if you played Jack Kennedy, you have to talk like Jack Kennedy, you know.

Mel   One easy question. Of all the regulars on your TV show, who would you say was the fastest wit in the group?

S.A.   That was probably Dayton Allen, although the word *wit* is a littler sharper to define than some forms of comedy, but it wasn't the kind of wit that Fred Allen had. It wasn't the kind that Groucho had or eventually had. Actually wit is very rare. Tom Poston, as I said, is a comedy actor and a wonderful one, but he didn't do wit for a living, and that's not a putdown, because some of our greatest American comedians had nothing to do with wit.

Jack Benny is uniformly beloved, even more by other comedians than by the public, perhaps, as much as he was loved, but he didn't have anything to say that his writers never told him, and there are some third-rate comics who are kind of witty, but you'll never care that much about them. It's just a separate way of making people laugh, the ability to quickly manipulate words and concepts.

Mel   Sort of like the way you always hear that among the Marx Brothers the funniest one was the least likely.

S.A.   The brothers used to claim it.

S.A.   I see. Well, then they'd know, sure. But Don Knotts also did not do wit. He had his own marvelous way of making us laugh. Louis Nye also does not do wit using the term in its common sense, but [he's] wonderfully funny. It was just his style, his cuckoo-ness, his bizarre approach to whatever he was talking about—still a very funny man. And Gabe [Dell] was funny in performance context, not just hanging around. He didn't say anything funny at the dinner table, so there's really no right way or wrong way. If people are laughing, then you've done your job.

Mel   Steve, three last questions, if we may. How is Jayne?

S.A.   She's fine. She's busily engaged here around the house at the moment that we had a gentleman in doing some heavy cleaning for us. I just got off a plane myself. I just came back from the Aspen, Colorado comedy festival where I taped a special with Rodney Dangerfield. That will be on the air in a couple of days.

Mel   Isn't that interesting. That leads into my next question. If you had any plans for another TV show or special.

S.A.   Well, there's just that one. I don't have plans for one of my own, but fortunately, the TV people call me constantly. We recently did a show with Larry—oh, God, I've forgotten the name of the famous guy.

Mel   Larry King?

S.A.   Larry King. Thank you. Don't tell him I drew a blank.

Mel   No, I won't.

S.A.   So they've rerun that about ten times recently, and I've been on the Dr. Katz show, and the Letterman show, the Leno show, the usual, you know, rounds.

S.A.   Somebody told me on the plane coming back today that the Rodney Dangerfield special will be on in just a few days. It's an HBO show, in case you were trying to track it down.

Mel   Oh, terrific. Yeah. We'll watch for that.

S.A.   Don't sit there with your grandchildren, however. The vulgarity is extreme, but a lot of funny people [are on the show].

Mel   Okay. Steve, one other thing I neglected to ask you. Did you write all of the *Meeting of the Minds* show [an educational program which aired originally on Public Broadcasting]?

S.A.   Yeah. The first year I wrote ninety-eight percent of the script. By the fourth year I was down to writing about seventy-five percent of the script, and I wanted to stop writing altogether and turn it over to other people, because it was an awful lot of work, but I never could find anybody else who could just take it over. But I was able to save myself work in two instances. There was a very clever fellow name Joe Early, who is generally speaking back from your general part of the country, and he was already doing a one-man show as Theodore Roosevelt, and then he did another one-man show as Ulysses S. Grant, so I took Joe's basic sketches, outlines, of those two characters and wove them in with three other participants, and then there was another fellow named—oh, dear, I've suddenly forgotten his name. Robert something. He was a concert violinist, who did a one-man show as Niccolo Paganini, so we took his basic act and wove it in with three other participants, and it was great television.

Mel   Do you have any personal favorite entertainers or favorite comedians who make you laugh?

S.A.   Well, my personal favorite, although I shy a little bit away from the word *favorite*, because it's easy to mention one name that you love, but then you sound like a dummy for saying—oh, you're ruling out so and so? You know, they may be even better, but you have personal preferences. Anyway, my personal favorite in the way he works is Sid Caesar, who I think is incredibly brilliant. In fact, we're talking now about my doing a special in which I pay tribute to him showing a lot of his old sketches, also some things I've written for him that he has done on other programs.

Mel   Oh, that would be great. He's one of my favorites.

S.A.   I love Sid's work. He's a truly creative genius of comedy.

Mel   Thank you so much, Steve, and it's been a pleasure and an honor talking with you.

S.A.   My pleasure indeed, Mel.

Perry Como

PIERINO RONALD "PERRY" COMO (MAY 18, 1912-MAY 12, 2001) was a much loved crooner, nightclub performer and television personality. Born in Canonsburg, Pennsylvania, he was a barber before signing on as a vocalist with the Ted Weems Orchestra in 1937. When the orchestra broke up in 1942, he went out on his own, becoming a major star on radio with *The Chesterfield Supper Club*. Perry signed with the RCA Victor label in 1943 and had hit after of hit during the forties and fifties: "Till the End of Time," Prisoner of Love," "Surrender," "Chi-Baba, Chi-Baba," "A-You're Adorable," "Some Enchanted Evening," "Hoop-De-Doo," "Don't Let the Stars Get in Your Eyes," "No Other Love," "Wanted," "Hot Diggity (Dog Ziggity Boom)," "Round and Round," and "Catch a Falling Star," (the latter being the Recording Industry Association of America's first official "Gold Record"). Perry Como's weekly television variety show set the standard for the genre and was one of the most successful programs in television history. After the show ended in 1964, "Mr. C" became the symbol of the Yuletide Season with his annual Christmas specials.

I had a wonderfully relaxed telephone conversation with this fine gentleman on November 21, 1997.

Mel   Hi, Perry, this is Mel Simons.

P.C.   Hi, Mel. How are you?

Mel   I'm good. How are you?

P.C.   Well, I'm half asleep.

Mel   Would this be a convenient time to ask you a few questions?

P.C.   Yes.

Mel   Perry, Cannonsberg, Pennsylvania, that's where you were born, am I correct?

P.C.   Yes, a hundred years ago!

Mel   Perry, you started out as a barber.

P.C.   Yup, I still am! I don't cut it well anymore. I used to.

Mel   If I flew down to Jupiter, Perry, would you give me a good deal on haircut?"

P.C.   Well, I don't charge anymore (Laughter).

Mel   Okay. I want to talk to you about your early career. Your first band was Freddie Carlane, am I correct?

P.C.   That's right. That's a long time ago.

Mel   Nineteen thirty-six or 'thirty-seven, your real big break was Ted Weems.

P.C.   Somewhere in there, yeah. The mid-thirties.

Mel   You also became a regular on *The Fibber McGee and Molly* radio show. Ted Weems was the bandleader. I believe that was the first time that you were heard n the radio.

P.C.   That's right. A long time ago. That's a hundred years ago, isn't it?

Mel   That was kind of your basic training on radio.

P.C.   Well, that's for sure. Fibber and Molly [Jim and Marion Jordan] were wonderful people. I haven't heard from them in years.

Mel   When you branched out on your own, Perry, how did you begin with RCA Victor Records?

P.C.   I haven't the vaguest idea how I got into that, but I've been with them for so many years now.

Mel   Over fifty years.

P.C.   At least that, yes. Your memory is pretty good.

Perry Como

Mel   You had many, many hit records, of course. Your first hit record was "Long Ago and Far Away."

P.C.   That's exactly right.

Mel   Your first No. 1 record was "Till the End of Time." That was based on Chopin, I believe.

P.C.   Oh, yes. That was a long time ago.

Mel   Nineteen forty-five, I believe, Perry. What were some of your personal favorite songs that you did?

P.C.   Well, you just mentioned one, "Till the End of Time." That was a great song for me. It was from an old classic.

Mel   Chopin

P.C.   Yup, Chopin is right.

Mel   Any other personal favorite songs that you enjoyed doing?

P.C.   All the million sellers, and thank God, I've had my share of them.

Mel   You know, Perry, I saw you perform twice in person at the South Shore Music Circus in Cohasset.

P.C.   Oh, yes. I remember. That was a long time ago. I was a young fellow!

Mel   I came backstage after the show. Scott Record, your opening act, introduced us. You did a nice tribute to Bing Crosby in your performance. Tell me about your relationship with Bing Crosby.

P.C.   Well, it's hard for some people to believe, but if it hadn't been for Bing, there wouldn't be any me. There wouldn't be any Andy Williams. There wouldn't be any of us. He was the beginning of that type of singing. Of course, Bing was a good friend, and I always kid him about it.

I'd say, "Bing, if it hadn't been for you, I'd still be cutting hair somewhere." And he'd get mad as hell at me.

Mel   I guess that Bing was the first of the crooners.

P.C.   Yes, the first and the best.

Mel   Well, I would argue that, Perry. I would say that you would be No. 1.

P.C.   You're very nice to say that, but I sang a little louder than he did, but that's about all (laughter).

Bing didn't like when I said he was the best. He said, "You do what you do, and I do what I do."

Mel   You were the two best crooners ever.

P.C.   Well, thank you, Mel. It's very nice of you to say that. I appreciate that. I still have to say that he was the best.

Mel   Perry, tell us about the Chesterfield show that you did for many years on radio.

P.C.   Well, it was the beginning of one of those things. There weren't too many shows on the air doing what we were doing. Chesterfield gave me the go ahead, and said, "Do what you want to do."

And it turned out beautifully for them and for me. For me, of course.

Mel   It was a wonderful show.

P.C.   Yes, it was. I had a lot of fun, and they were very lenient as far as what I did on the show. I told them, I said, "Look, you know what I do. Is this what you want?"

They said, "Yes. That's what we want," so it was a nice association. They were wonderful people, too.

Mel   Did you smoke Chesterfield?

P.C.   Ah, yes (laughter). I used to get them by the case. I became very popular in the neighborhood, giving out cigarettes! (laughter)

Mel   Now, Perry, that, of course, led into your wonderful television show. Tell me how that began.

P.C.   Well, I really don't know how it began. But it was a great thing for me. I think at that time we were the only ones on the air! Television and me got along very well. People liked what they saw.

Mel   People *loved* what they saw.

P.C.   Well, they knew I could always give them a haircut, you know (laughter).

Mel   Perry, those were all live shows. Am I correct?

P.C.   Oh, yes. And I think that's what made it a good show. If something screwed up, I had the fortune of being able to say something funny, rather than have it a big mistake, and the guest like that. They said, "Well, this guy is crazy."

        And, of course, all Italians are a little crazy (laughter).

Mel   Did you enjoy television as much as radio?

P.C.   Yes, but there was more work in television than in radio. At the end we started to do the show on tape, and it lost something, you know. They start fixing. Once you start fixing, I think you lose your continuity. The spontaneity is gone. If you made a mistake, you said it.

        Once it got on tape, then it has to be perfect and all that stuff, you know.

Mel   Your Christmas specials were fabulous. Tell me about how those developed.

P.C.   Well, that was the work of a lot of people, you know, a director, a producer, writers. I have to say that they knew what I was capable of doing. We never did anything above it or beneath it. People liked it, so we were in good shape.

Mel   I was wondering, since the program was live in the beginning, can you remember anything going wrong that really surprised you? Any funny incidents?

P.C.   I don't remember too many things going right (laughter).

Mel   What did you enjoy the most, radio, television, records or live audiences?

P.C.   Well, I had such a nice thing going with people, live audiences to me was the most fun. You know, I could screw up, and the audience would just look at me and laugh. You can't do that on television.

Mel   Perry, I want to thank you very, very much. You are one of the greatest singers ever, and one of the great personalities in the history of show business.

P.C.   Thank you, Mel. I'm glad to hear that, even at my age. Please call me again, and if you ever want a good haircut, Mel, come see me in Jupiter!

Gale Storm

Gale Storm

JOSEPHINE OWAISSA COTTLE (B. APRIL 5, 1922) is an actress, television personality and singer. As a youngster, her two loves were dancing and ice skating. Her family moved to California and she was given the name "Gale Storm" upon her arrival in Hollywood in 1940. After receiving some valuable training in B-movies for Monogram Pictures, she became one of the first major television stars, in the popular sitcoms *My Little Margie* and *The Gale Storm Show/Oh! Suzanna*. She also topped the charts with several 'fifties-era pop songs, including the million-seller "I Hear You Knockin.'" While *My Little Margie* lived on in reruns, the star was in demand as a game show panelist, a Las Vegas headliner and the lead in numerous stage plays. I had the pleasure of interviewing this talented lady by telephone in front of a live audience on May 22, 2000 ...

G.S.   Hello?

Mel   Gale?

G.S   Yes.

Mel   Mel Simons.

G.S.   Hi, Mel.

Mel   How are you?

G.S.   Fine. How are you?

Mel   I'm fine, Gale.

G.S.   Well, that's nice.

Mel   And I'd like to talk a little bit about your great career.

G.S.   All righty. I'll try for answers then. You can ask the questions, but I may not have the answers.

Mel   I reread your book last night, by the way. I've read it twice and enjoyed it immensely both times.

G.S.   Oh, thank you.

Mel   Born in Bloomington and then settled in Houston.

G.S.   Yeah, I never did see Bloomington.

Mel   How old were you when you moved?

G.S.   Just knew Texas, of course.

Mel   Yeah. Yeah.

G.S.   Burlington, Texas.

Mel   Are they near each other, by the way, Bloomington—

G.S.   No, they're not. Bloomington is sort of in the middle. I've just looked at it on the map, and I never went back after I guess about six months. That's why I'm not very familiar with it.

Mel   I understand. And you tell in the book, you know, how you did a lot of musicals—

G.S.   Right.

Mel   —in school, but—

G.S.   Oh, musicals in schools?

Mel   In school, yeah.

G.S.   No, I really didn't do that many musicals in school. I just did plays and things like that.

Mel   Oh, I see.

G.S.   I didn't start any of my singing stuff until much later.

Mel   What about the dancing?

G.S.   No, I didn't have any of that because, well, for one thing my family wasn't well fixed financially, and so I did not have an opportunity to take dancing lessons or singing things, so I didn't have that until I started to do it professionally, which means I didn't do it too well, but I loved it anyway.

Mel   Oh, I understand. You tell in the book the big break was Jesse Lasky.

G.S.   Yes.

Mel   Gateway to Hollywood. Could you relate that story to us?

G.S.   Right. Uh-huh. Jesse Lasky was a very well-known Hollywood producer, and he and his entourage toured the United States looking for talent in all the different states to bring to Hollywood to compete in a series of radio shows, Sunday radio shows that would—I'm getting in the middle of my story without making it clean.

Anyway, so when Jesse Lasky came to Houston where I was in high school, and I probably wouldn't have entered the contest. I wouldn't have had that much confidence nor even have dreamed that I could ever aspire, you know, to be an actress, but I had these two wonderful school teachers, Miss Oatman and Miss Collier. They were my English teacher and my Latin teacher, and they just told me that I was going to do that, you know, because as you said, I had always been active in dramatics in school and everything, and they just thought I should, and I just kept saying, "Well, no, I can't do that." And they said, "Oh, yes, you are."

Anyway, those two teachers changed my life, because they saw to it that I went and I entered the contest, and then I was selected as a winner in Houston and was taken to Hollywood to compete in the finals. It was a wonderful contest. It was a one-hour radio show, a big radio show on Sundays, and they would present the contestants, like three sets, you know, a boy and a girl, three different sets of boys and girls, and they'd have a Hollywood star, a big star that would perform in the play things that we did along with us, and from the very beginning of the contest, when Jesse Lasky toured the United States, he had the names selected in advance, and the value to that was that each time the radio show went out on Sunday, he would say who will be the next Gale Storm and the boy's name was Terry Belmont.

Yeah, and so anyway, I was brought up from Houston as a contestant, and it was strictly acting. It was not——

Mel   No singing?

G.S.   No. Uh-uh. And so I won the contest, and as I said, it was a wonderful contest because many times you win a contest but you don't win anything, and this one was worked out so beautifully. It was CBS and sponsored by Wrigley Company, as I said, and they saw to it that we won contracts with RKO studios, which of course was a big studio then, and when you signed a contract, it's like a seven-year contract, which is kind of a joke, because at the end of six months if they wish they can drop your option.

Well, the contest had stipulated that they could not, let's say, just keep us six months and not have us do anything, and then drop our options, so they said that they had to have used us, not in the same picture, but used us in a good part in a picture or they could not drop the option.

So it was a real fair contest. You know, just really, really well thought out and well done.

Mel   And did that ultimately led to you doing movies?

G.S.   Doing what?

Mel   Movies?

G.S.   I'm sorry?

Mel   Motion pictures?

G.S.   Oh, yes.

Mel   Yeah. I think I'm too close, Gale. I'll back off a bit.

G.S.   Yes. I was getting a whining or something.

Mel   Yes, I think we're okay now.

G.S.   You were singing to me or something there.

Mel   Yes. I think we got it straightened out. What were some of the early movies that you did?

G.S.   Oh, my goodness, you really wouldn't — Well, I guess with my career I guess I feel like God just kind of picked me up by the scruff of the neck, you know, and put me where I should be and put me in Hollywood, and I hadn't stopped to think that my Texas accent was going to be a real problem at the time. Everybody else had an accent, I think, but anyway, when I won the contest, the day that I won the contest, there were two producers that were there, and they had planned this out. I knew nothing about it, but they had decided it would be a good publicity thing to say that they were going to use me in their movie *Tom Brown's School Days*, which was aside from the one that I was supposed to do where they had to give me a part, you know—a good part.

So, anyway, the wonderful thing about—you know, God took care of that too, because if I hadn't have had that I wouldn't have been—I was tutored for like, oh, let me see, it must have been at least six weeks for an English accent, and being tutored for an English accent put it overboard enough that I could see and I could correct my Texas accent to a pretty good degree, so that was very important. That was the most important thing about that picture, *Tom Brown's School Days*. I played a twelve-year-old girl in it, and then they also, the picture that they used me in at RKO was called *One Crowded Night*, which you would not have heard of necessarily, but it was a good part, and actually it was a good picture.

Mel   Tell us about your association with Roy [Rogers]. How was he to work with?

G.S.   Oh, he was wonderful. He just is—you know, he is just as real and just as good a person as you'd ever want to think. He was just a joy to work with. Very professional, of course, but just as friendly and nice and sweet and full of fun as he could be. It was always real fun when he'd come in. In makeup in the morning he'd tease all the girls and everything, and he was just really neat.

Mel   In the book you tell a delightful story about your horse and Trigger. Could you—

G.S.   (Laughter) I'm really sorry.

Mel   It's a lovely story.

G.S.   Being from Texas you're supposed to be fairly comfortable with horses, and I just was not, and I was so scared every time I'd have to ride. I would do it really well, because I didn't want to have to do it twice, you know.

Mel   Yes.

G.S.   And so I had this one scene where Roy is feisty with gorgeous Trigger, and I'm on the horse that's supposed to be as steady as they could make it for me to make me comfortable, and we were riding along in the back of the truck that's pulling the camera, and we're riding along the trail, and Roy, of course, is singing to me, and, you know, we're follow-ing the truck, and I'm looking, of courses, enamored of his singing, no doubt, but the truck didn't really show—the camera didn't show the horses' heads, and they just were on us, and Trigger would just—at every opportunity Trigger would reach over and nip my horse in the neck, and my horse would shy, which would scare me to pieces, so that was the most memorable horse ride I ever had.

Mel   I'll bet. You also mentioned that there were several Triggers, which I was not aware of.

G.S.   Oh, yeah. I don't know. I really don't know how many, but I know there were more than one. There had to be, you know.

Mel   Now, after the three movies you did with Roy Rogers, then what did you do in movies?

G.S.   Oh, well, then I was signed to a contract at Monogram, which was a small studio, and they made what we called B-pictures then. You know, they'd have a double feature, and they'd have the more expensive pic-ture, you know, would be the A-picture, and then they'd have the lower-budgeted pictures, the B-pictures, and so that was just wonderful for me, too, because for one thing, of course, by then I was married, and I was just practically the only person they had there, so they used me all the time, and it was just wonderful, a wonderful, a wonderful experi-ence, because for one thing, some of the pictures were six-day pictures. In fact, I did one that they didn't finish but they released anyway. I survived, of course, but—

Mel   Now, what led you into getting the role in *My Little Margie* on TV?

G.S.   Oh, well, nothing really led me into it. In fact, that was always kind of a mystery to me, because I really had not—I had gotten attention in Hollywood mostly for dramatic parts, you know, rather than for comedy. I had been doing comedy pictures, you know, and I knew that I kind of had a flair for comedy, but anyway, and my career was kind of at a—well, it wasn't exactly booming along and I had this call at home from a producer, Hal Roach, Jr., whom I had never met, and ordinarily they would call your agent, you know, but instead they called me. My agent went with me and everything, but anyway, they said they had a script written for a television show called *My Little Margie* and that they had Charlie Farrell for it, and they wanted me to come in so that they could see how they felt about me, and if they liked me for it, then I could see how I felt about doing it.

So anyway, I went in and they gave me a script, and I went home and I read it, and I can't be explicit about it, but I just—I felt like—and I wasn't in a position to be choosey, you know or picky about things, but I felt like the father/daughter relationship wasn't really as healthy as it should be. I don't know if I felt like they weren't nice enough to each other or what, but so I kind of had my nerve, and I called up and I said—I told them why—I said, "I want to thank you for giving me the opportunity, but I don't feel right about it," because of that, and I didn't expect to hear from them anymore, and I guess in a couple of weeks they called and said they had rewritten the script and would I come in again and get it, and I never did know why Hal Roach, Jr. wanted me. You know, it wasn't like I was —It was just one of those things. There again, I guess God made up His mind what I was supposed to do, and so when I went in and got the script and I love it. I just thought it was great.

Mel   It clicked right from the start, didn't it?

G.S.   Well, it was funny, because we were a summer replacement for *I Love Lucy.*

Mel   Mondays at nine.

G.S.   *I Love Lucy* was very well established, you know, and loved.

Mel   Sure.

G.S.   And that was supposed to be like the kiss of death. You know, you can't really go in and substitute very well for something that everybody loves. They don't want you; they want *that*, which of course isn't true. But then we only had—It was supposed to require thirteen episodes in order to establish your characterizations, and we only had nine, because that's when they came back, you know, Lucy came back from their hiatus after nine episodes, and I was supposed to make it, so it wasn't going to work, and then the critics did not exactly embrace it. They were not unkind at all to me or anything, but they just didn't think it would work, so anyway it ended up with the critics saying: "Nobody liked it but the people."

Mel   So true, and you did 126—

G.S.   So that was sufficient, of course.

Mel   Yeah. And you did 126 episodes.

G.S.   You bet, yeah.

Mel   Now, you know what's interesting, Gale, many radio shows turned to television. With you it happened in the reverse, didn't it?

G.S.   Yeah. I think that's really kind of unique.

Mel   How did the radio version start?

G.S.   Well, we were still, of course, shooting the television show, which was a heavy schedule, and so Hal Roach Jr. came in on the set and talked to Charlie and to me, Charlie Farrell and to me, and he said, "with CBS…"—it was a CBS show—and he said, "CBS wants a radio show [version of] *Margie*, and we said, "*When?*" You know, like, when are you going to do it, because you're working all week long, you know, and so Howell said, "Sundays."

Mel   Wow.

G.S.   So that's what we did, and the radio show had, the only two characters in *My Little Margie* on the radio show that were the same were Charlie Farrell and me, and the others were all radio actors, which was kind of interesting.

Mel   Did you enjoy doing radio?

G.S.   Oh, I loved it, yeah. It was fun. We had an audience, and you got the audience response, and you didn't have to memorize lines. It was just, you know, it was a piece of cake. It was great. You know, the people were good and the scripts were good.

Mel   Oh, yeah. Charles Farrell was from this area, Gale. He was from Walpole, Massachusetts.

G.S.   I always thought of him as being from Boston.

Mel   Yeah, well, Walpole is just—

G.S.   That's close enough.

Mel   Close enough. Oh, yeah.

G.S.   He would always say [with a Boston accent] "Margie."

Mel   Yeah, Margie, right. He was pretty successful in silent movies, wasn't he?

G.S.   Oh, yeah. Well, not only silent. He was pretty good in others, too.

Mel   Talking movies also. I didn't' realize that he had done talking movies as well. I thought just silents Charlie had done.

G.S.   No, I'm sure he'd done others. I'm really not absolutely certain to say that. I don't know why.

Mel   When did *My Little Margie* leave the air?

G.S.   Well, we started shooting it in 1952, and it went right—as we shot them, it went on.

Mel   And when was the last show done, what year?

G.S.   Oh, well, it was I guess about—it was four years, four and a half, close to four and a half years.

Mel   Pretty good run, Gale.

G.S.   You bet.

Mel   How much time elapsed between *My Little Margie*—

G.S.   And *The Gale Storm Show/ Oh Susanna*?

Mel   Exactly.

G.S.   One year.

Mel   Tell us about that. How did that develop?

G.S.   After, when I finished *My Little Margie*, and I loved it, of course, but it was really, really hard work in every way. You know, it was demanding physically, mentally, emotionally. It really was, and the hours were long, and so I said when I finished *Margie*, I said, "I'm never going to do another television series, unless it's something I can't resist," and so people would call during that year, and it was wonderful that year in between, because I found out what television can do for you, because the fact that *Margie* had been a successful show and people liked it, I got to do all kinds of wonderful things like guest spots on all the big shows. I got to sing, you know, on all the big—be a guest, and sing a couple of songs on everything.

Mel   Some of the shows you did—I got this right out of your book, but I'd like you to comment on some of the variety shows that you did. Let's talk about Perry Como.

G.S.   Oh, Perry Como, I guess I did about—I don't remember for sure—two or three. I know I did more than one, but I'm not sure if I did three, but I know it was two because I had a hit record out then. I had the hit record, "I Hear You Knockin'." It's the one I have a gold record for.

Mel   Oh, yeah.

G.S.   It was the first one I've ever recorded and everything, so anyway, that's what they wanted was because it was a hit record, so I sang "I Hear You Knockin'" and that was one I liked. I liked that a lot, and then when they invited me back for the second time, I had another record out that I wanted to do, and I went to this producer, and I said—because they had said they wanted me to do "*I Hear You Knockin'*" and I said, "Well, I know, but I've got this record that's really good I want you to hear. Anyway, that's where I found out who really made the decisions on the show.

Mel   It was Perry.

G.S.   Perry Como, and all the directors said, "Well, I don't know." And the producer said, "Well, I don't know." Anyway, it ended up that I asked Perry Como if he'd let me sing the other song instead, and he said, "No. I want you to do "I Hear You Knockin'."

Mel   And that's what you did.

G.S.   And I said, "But..." you know, and I gave him my little sales pitch, and he said, "I know, but I want you to do "I Hear You Knockin'.""

Mel   Yeah, and when the boss says "do it," *you do it*.

G.S.   Yeah, you betcha. It was his show.

Mel   Right.

G.S.   You know, he was just as dear as he could be, but a very strong person, really. You know, you think of him as so laid back and easy, but he knew what he wanted.

Mel   And how. And he was loved.

G.S.   Oh, yes. He was, yes.

Mel   Now, you tell a lovely story [in your book]. This really broke me up. Would you tell the Milton Berle story that you told in the book?

G.S.   Well, I—

Mel   Oh, you can tell us. It's just between us, Gale.

G.S.   Oh, of course. I mean—

Mel   It won't go any further.

G.S.   You and me, right?

Mel   Right. You have my word.

G.S.   Well, you know it's funny, because I see him now. In fact, for several years I've seen him in the different things that we go to, you know, that he and his wife are always there, and he's a nice man, but when I did that show with him, he was such a prima donna, and he would march back and forth with a towel around his neck, and I can't even remember explicitly what bothered me. It shouldn't have bothered me whatever he did, but it was –it just wasn't as pleasant an experience as I'd hoped

for, you know, and I'd had really good experiences on all of the wonderful guest shows or the shows I got to guest on.

Mel   Yeah

G.S.   And so anyway, I did his show, and then I did a Bob Hope show, and I
        don't know what was going on with him, then. I had a real good song.
        I had "Silver Bells," and we sang together, and then I forget, but one I
        sang by myself in production, and that was lovely, but that was not
        exactly—that was not as pleasant a show to do.

Mel   Well, I think I know what you're talking about, you know, having read
        your book twice where you tell about —

G.S.   Then you can probably tell me.

Mel   In the book you basically said you weren't sure when to come out with
        him, and you asked him and he didn't answer you, and you put your
        arm in his, and he just walked on stage without you.

G.S.   That's right, and he would not accept my arm.

Mel   Amazing.

G.S.   That was just strange. I just didn't understand. See, I don't know what
        was going on with him personally, of course, you know, why he reacted
        that way, and I don't know what I would have done, and I'm sure I didn't,
        but anyway, I told my agent after that. I said, "I don't want to do any guest
        spots for comedians." I said, "They're so…" You know, I don't need that.
        That's okay, and so then my agent said, "They want you for Jack Benny.

Mel   That's exactly what I was going to ask you, Gale. Tell us about Jack.

G.S.   Oh, no. I said, "No, that's another comedian, and I don't care how good
        he is, and all that, but I don't want to do." And so anyway, my agent
        said, "Well…" Anyway, he talked me into it, and I am so glad I did that,
        because that was—That man was just the most delightful experience.

        The other shows, you know, when you start out you sit around all the
        people who are in the show. You sit around a table and you read the script,
        and the other shows nobody said a word other than what they were sup-
        posed to read, you see. Nobody offered to—And the words *yes man* and

stuff, and I couldn't believe it. I sat down, and we started to read around with Jack Benny, and everybody could say, "Hey, why don't we try this," or "Do you think my line would be better if I...." whatever, and Jack Benny was just, you know, an open, wonderful loving and caring man, you know, who's one of the funniest people you would ever, ever enjoy in your life, so I had a song to sing that was kind of rangy. It was "You Make Me Feel So Young," and I had Nelson Riddle to do the arrangement, which was just heavenly, but I was nervous about it, because it was a very "rangy" song, and I thought, *What am I going to do if I crackle on that top note? I'm going to want to die at least,* you know, so they knew that—I guess I had made it a little bit clear that I was a little nervous about it, and so when I was waiting to go on, I was waiting in the wings for my cue, and Jack Benny came up and put his arm around me, and he said, "You're gonna be great," and that just dissolved me. That was just the sweetest, dearest thing in the world.

Mel He always had the reputation for being one of the nicest people in show business.

G.S. Oh, he is. He is just—you know, I just cried when he died. I just cried.

Mel Yeah. It was a very sad day for us all. On *Oh, Susanna* the thing I remember, Gale, is that every third show was a musical.

G.S. Right.

Mel Which you must have loved.

G.S. Oh, I did. That's the one way they got me to—you know, I said I would never do it again unless I can't resist it. Well, that's what I couldn't resist was the fact that every third show was musical, and I'd get to do production numbers and pre-record and sing really great songs, great standards and stuff, you know.

Mel Which brings me to my next question, Gale. The amount of Top Ten records that you had is amazing. I'm going to start with your first hit, which was "I Hear You Knockin'." It was a No. 2 record. It was No. 2 for weeks, and it was on the charts for an amazing amount of weeks—seventeen weeks!

G.S. Uh-huh.

Mel And you got the gold record for that, am I right?

G.S.   Yes.

Mel   Your next record hit No. 6 on the top 10, "Teenage Prayer."

G.S.   See, you know more about it than I do.

Mel   And the next one is really amazing, because Dean Martin had a No. 1 record. It was the biggest hit he ever had, "Memories Are Made of This."

G.S.   Right.

Mel   And you had a No. 5 record with the same song.

G.S.   Yeah. That's a good song.

Mel   Oh, what a great song!

G.S.   Great song, you betcha.

Mel   It's amazing, you did all these wonderful songs, many of them were cover records, you know, done by other people—

G.S.   That's right, uh-huh.

Mel   —but you had big hits. The next song you had was a No. 9 record on the charts for 14 weeks, "Why do Fools Fall In Love?" and Frankie Lyman and the Teenagers recorded that.

G.S.   Yeah.

Mel   Then you had a No. 6 record with "Ivory Tower."

G.S.   Yeah.

Mel   Was it Cathy Carr who had the record?

G.S.   I don't know. Isn't that awful that I don't?

Mel   I think it was Cathy Carr, and then Bonnie Guitar wrote and recorded a song, and her version only hit No. 19, and you hit No. 4 with "Dark Moon."

G.S.   "Dark Moon" was the one by—When I started recording, I didn't know what a cover record was. I didn't know "I Hear You Knockin'" was a cover record until I heard them comparing it with Smiley Lewis's original one, and then they said, "Yeah, it's out, this other singer's," so anyway I was doing the cover records, but when I got to the one, the "Dark Moon" with Bonnie Guitar, and I heard—I didn't always hear the cover record, because I did my version of it.

For instance, one that we did all have to listen to was Why Do Fools Fall in Love?—because we couldn't understand the words.

Mel   Yeah, I remember.

G.S.   We had to slow it down to make sure we had the right words, but with the Bonnie Guitar one, and I thought her record was great, and I knew she had written it, and so that was the only time I sort of rebelled and I said, "I'm not going to do that. I'm not going to cover this record. I'm not going to do it unless Bonnie Guitar comes to me and says she wants me to do it." And so that's what they did. They got Bonnie Guitar to come to me and say it would be good for her, you know, if I would do it, and so I did.

Mel   And you had the bigger hit of the two.

G.S.   Yeah, but it was good for her both ways, because it gave her more since she had written the song.

Mel   What was your favorite, Gale, of all the songs you recorded?

G.S.   You know, I never had a favorite of anything. Isn't that funny, but I just don't. It's like– maybe that's like saying "Which of your children is your favorite?" There are just so many things that I loved doing, and I just can't have a favorite.

Mel   We tried to get you I guess about two or three months ago, and you were not available because you were going to some sort of a testimonial for ZaSu Pitts.

G.S.   Yes.

Mel   Which led me to believe that you had a wonderful warm relationship with her.

G.S.   Oh, yes.

Mel   Tell us about ZaSu.

G.S.   Oh, she was wonderful. She, as you know, we were — I guess you'd call
        her my sidekick, but she was more than that in *Oh Susannah.* She was
        born in Parsons, Kansas, and so Parsons, Kansas, started—I guess they
        had two years prior to this year where they had had a ZaSu Pitts film
        festival, and they honored her, and had all of her pictures that they showed
        and stuff like that, and so they had asked me the year before to come, and
        I couldn't because I had a conflict. I had something else I was doing, and
        so I'd known a year—so I said, "But I'll do it next time," so I had known
        a year in advance that I was going to do this.

        And Parsons, Kansas, is not a big city, you know. It's just a small town, and
        they had had a tornado the week before I went there that really, really did
        some damage. I'd never seen anything like that before, but anyway, Par-
        sons, Kansas, has the nicest people in the whole wide world. I had the best
        time. Everything that they had arranged there was just—everything was so
        well done and just beautifully put together, and I was so—it was just a joy
        from the word "go," and of course, ZaSu—working with her—I had just,
        of course, just loved her. She was a wonderful person as well as being a
        delight and a very funny, funny woman, and she made these handkerchiefs
        that were like a-well, I can't point over the radio, you know, can't show you
        how wide they were, but they were big handkerchiefs, and she'd hand-
        rolled the hems on them, and she would carry one of those. You know, her
        hands were just living objects, because she would just fling those hands
        around, and if you'd seen her, you'd know exactly what I mean.

Mel   I was always a fan of hers.

G.S.   Oh, yeah.

Mel   She always seemed to play an older woman, even when she was younger,
        she played an older —

G.S.   Well, that was just—you know, she started out as a very dramatic actress.

Mel   Oh!

Mel   Now, Gale, if I'm not out of line with this, you tell me. In your book
        you talk very honestly and openly about your alcohol situation.

G.S.   Right.

Mel   Could you tell us how that started and how you eventually conquered it?

G.S.   How I *what*?

Mel   How you *conquered* it?

G.S.   Oh, well, I guess I never felt like I conquered it. I felt like I could not,
         I could *not* conquer it. God had to do that for me, because I had
         proved to myself I could not do it myself.

Mel   How did it begin, Gale?

G.S.   You know, I know some people, I think it's a comfort to some people
         who are alcoholics to be able to say, *Well, I wouldn't have had this
         problem if—but it started after my husband left me, after my child died,
         my whatever.* You know, in other words, they could attach the onset to
         some experience that was bad—like *that* caused it.

         Well, it doesn't really cause it, because if you're an alcoholic, it is going to
         emerge at some time or another. You don't have to have any reason,
         because that's the chemistry in your body. It's just different from people
         who are not alcoholics, and so mine, it was just very, very—it was just
         very gradual, and of course, very gradually, but it becomes a terrible
         problem very gradually, and then it's not so gradual anymore. It gets just
         really, really frightening and really, really bad, and I prayed.

         You know, I guess I knew that God was going to help me. I just didn't know
         when, and so anyway I've had a really, really rough, bad time, and my husband
         was wonderfully supportive and my family, and it was such a stigma for women
         then, that you didn't want anybody to know it, and of course, I never ever
         would drink before I did anything professionally, and I would fortify myself
         before we went out socially so that I wouldn't drink too much. You know, I
         didn't want anybody to know, in other words. It was like a horrible secret, and
         so when I finally found this hospital where they treated alcoholism—*only* alco-
         holism—and I went there, and I didn't want anybody to know, you know, that
         I was in there and but after I started to learn about it and learn that it's not a
         character weakness. It's not like lack of willpower. It's a *disease*, and [I] was
         educated about it, and it just worked for me so beautifully, and once I found
         that out, all I wanted was to share [the information with others].

         No longer did I feel like I don't want anybody to know that I was an
         alcoholic. I wanted everybody to know, who was hurting, everybody out
         there who was hurting like I had. I wanted them to know there was help,

and so I asked the people at this hospital that I was in. I said, "Do you ever do commercials?" and they said, "Yes." And I said, "Well, I'd like to do one," and they said "No." Because they said for one thing, you know, actresses can be famous for announcing that they're cured and they're fine, and then later on relapse, and that's very bad for them. You know, it looks bad for them. It looks bad for the hospital, so they said they just didn't want me to do that, and so I had to work real hard. I had to beg them to let me do it, and they did, and that was just about the most important thing I felt like I could ever have done, because I got to say, you know, in this commercial I did, and not just one, but I did several after that, and I got to say, "There is help. I'm an alcoholic, and I know that there are people out there who are hurting, and who have loved ones who are hurting, and there is a way out of there. Anyway, there is help." And that was just about the most satisfying thing I ever could have done.

Mel   Yeah. Very, very inspiring, Gale.

G.S.   It was just—it was great, because I felt as if —When I was finished with that I felt as if God had given me a contract saying, "You will never ever have to worry or be concerned about alcoholism again." I've never had a moment of temptation or having to be aware of things like you can be. Many times, you know, a person has real problems afterwards.

Mel   How long have you been alcohol-free now, Gale?

G.S.   Oh, let me see. I think I have — I should know exactly. I believe it was my 21st birthday. I'm 21 years old. I look older, but I'm not.

Mel   What do you think of that, everybody? Twenty-one years!

(Applause)

G.S.   Yes, twenty-one years.

Mel   Boy, oh boy. Very inspirational, Gale!

G.S.   It's like with the kids, I'm not sure how old my kids are, but I can tell you when they were born. It was 1979 in February, that's when I was explicit I was sober, you know, free of alcoholism, and it's just been just a joy ever since.

Mel   Well, Gale, you've been just wonderful.

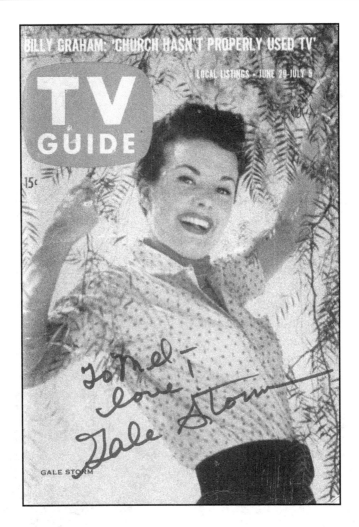

G.S.   Yep. And I've had a good time.

Mel   Everybody loves you, Gale.

G.S.   Thank you. I just appreciate that so much.

Mel   Thanks a million. You've been an absolute delight. I appreciate everything.

G.S.   Well, Mel, you've made it the way it is, and I appreciate that.

Mel   Thank you, Gale. I'll be taking to you soon.

G.S.   Thanks, Mel. Bye-bye.

Soupy Sales

Soupy Sales

MILTON SUPMAN (B. JANUARY 8, 1926) is a popular comedian and actor. He received his unusual nickname from his family; his brothers were known as "Hambone" and "Chicken Bone"—and Milton was dubbed "Soup Bone," which was later shortened to "Soupy." While working as a professional disc jockey, he chose the surname "Sales" after the comedian Chic Sale. Soupy started doing comedy while he was a student at Marshall College, where he was majoring in journalism. He did several television shows in Cincinnati and Detroit before going to New York. Known as "The King of Silliness," he achieved lasting fame as the host of the long-running daily television children's show, *Lunch with Soupy Sales*. During the course of that show, he was hit in the face with thousands of cream pies. On a more serious note, he had a career as a recording artist; his biggest hit was "The Mouse." He was later in demand on the television game-show circuit.

I had the pleasure of interviewing Soupy on October 20, 2006.

Mel   I'm so happy to be sitting here with one of television's great stars, Soupy Sales. Soupy, it's great to see you.

S.S.   Thank you, Mel. It's a pleasure to be with you.

Mel   You have always been an idol of mine. Soupy, even though so many people identify you with New York City I don't think you're from New York originally, are you?

S.S.   No, no, no. I wasn't born in New York. I was born in Franklinton, North Carolina. When I was very young we moved to Huntington, West Virginia.

        My first major market was on the radio in Cincinnati. I then also did TV in Cincinnati. I then did two television shows in Detroit. One

107

was a kid's show and the other was a teen dance show. Then I did a nighttime talk show where jazz musicians would come on and play.

Mel   So, basically did you interview these musicians, Soupy, in addition to their playing?

S.S.   Yes

Mel   Were there any name people that we would know?

S.S.   Everybody. From Chet Baker to Dizzy Gillespie. Everybody did the show.

Mel   You know, Soupy, this is a whole new side that I'm seeing of you. I don't associate you at all with jazz. Are you a jazz lover, personally?

S.S.   Yes, I am.

Mel   Did you grow up listening and enjoying jazz?

S.S.   Yes, I did.

Mel   Well, very interesting. Now, what was your big break? What started you off in New York?

S.S.   Well, in Los Angeles it became hip to get hit with a pie by Soupy Sales. I was doing a show called *Lunch with Soupy Sales* in L.A. The big names would come in to get hit with a pie!

Mel   Who were some of the big names who got hit?

S.S.   Oh, Frank Sinatra, Burt Lancaster and many others. So then I came to New York in September, 1964. My New York show on Channel 5 started.

Mel   What station is that in New York?

S.S.   It was WNEW-TV, Channel 5, at 205 E. 67th Street.

Mel   Now, tell me about your show in New York when it first started. What was the show like? Did it start with the pies or did that come later?

S.S.   It started with the pies. And from that it just grew. You know what really helped me take off in New York? It was a live show at the Paramount Theatre. It was Easter, 1965.

Mel   What was that show like at the Paramount? I mean, did you throw pies in the theatre?

S.S.   No, there were no pies thrown in the theatre. I introduced the song, "The Mouse." There were a lot of other artists on the bill with me—The Hollies, Little Richard, Shirley Ellis. Big names at the time. There were so many people standing in line that it made all the newspapers. It was amazing.

Mel   I have an album of you, Soupy, of you singing. Just straight singing, and you absolutely knocked me out as to what a terrific singer you are. Are most people aware that you are a legit singer?

S.S.   No, I don't think so. It's very exciting to hear that. I always loved to sing.

Mel   I have an album of standards. It's so out of context for you as everybody associates you with your craziness and your pie throwing. But, let me tell you, Soupy, you are one dynamite singer.

S.S.   Thank you so much.

Mel   Now, here's a question you've probably been asked every day of your life: Approximately how many pies have you thrown and how many pies have you received?

S.S.   I received more than I threw. Most of them were thrown at me. I received about twenty-two thousand pies!

Mel   Of course, the classic story that is always told the New Year's story. I've heard you tell it many times, and I love it. Tell the famous New Year's Day story.

S.S.   There were just a couple of minutes left in the show. I looked at the camera and I said, "Kids, mom and dad are tired. They were out late last night. Would you tiptoe in the bedroom. Don't wake them up. They are still sleeping. Get your dad's wallet and take out those little green pieces of paper with pictures on them, and send them to me."

And this is the part nobody ever gets right. I then said, "I'll send you a postcard from Puerto Rico!" And then I got hit with a pie. And then I got hit with a suspension!

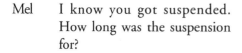

Mel   I know you got suspended. How long was the suspension for?

S.S.   It was for one week.

Mel   And approximately how much money was sent in? Did you ever get a figure?

S.S.   Around eighty-eight dollars.

Mel   Soupy, we'll wind it up with one last question. How many years were you on television, and any special memories from all the years you entertained us?

S.S.   So many years and so many wild times. I loved Sinatra and Sammy Davis, Jr. They were memorable.

Mel   Tell me about Sinatra and Sammy Davis.

S.S.   Well, Sinatra did the show twice.

Mel   Did Sinatra request to get hit with a pie?

S.S.   Oh, yes. It was his idea. It was so funny because nobody expected it. It came as a great surprise.

Mel   He was pleased with the outcome?

S.S.   Oh, yes.

Mel   Did Sammy Davis, Jr. get hit with a pie?

S.S.   Oh, yes. He came on all dressed up. He didn't believe in wearing old clothes. We said, "You better change your clothes." He said, "No, I like it this way."

He got hit with a pie and he loved it. He was wonderful. He was lovely. What a sense of humor he had.

Mel   Soupy, it's been wonderful interviewing you. Thank you so much.

S.S.   Thank you for your time. I hope we'll do it again.

Soupy Sales and Mel Simons

Joe Franklin

Joe Franklin

JOSEPH FORTGANG (B. MARCH 9, 1926) is a legendary New York radio and television personality. During the forty-three-year run of *The Joe Franklin Show*, he interviewed an estimated 10,000 guests. Joe introduced many bright new talents on his program, but his favorite guests seemed to be the show business heroes of his youth. So often did he present these former stars to a new audience that he became known as "The King of Nostalgia," (a term he claimed to have invented). After having appeared on Joe's television many times through the years, I was honored to have him as an interview subject on October 22, 2006.

Mel   I'm so happy to be interviewing Joe Franklin!

       Joe, I started off as a fan of yours, and then I had the pleasure of being on your TV show many, many times.

J.F.   Many times, right.

Mel   And it was always a delight being with you. We talked about old-time radio and old-time television.
       We are going to get into your show, your wonderful television show. How did it all begin for you, the origin of your TV work?

J.F.   Well, I began on radio. I was a record picker for a man named Martin Block. It was a program called *The Make Believe Ballroom*. I was about sixteen or seventeen years old. He then got me my own radio show because he liked me. In fact, he said to me, "Joe, don't compete with me," as if anybody could compete with him, because he was the king of all the new records.

So, I went out and I started to collect some old records. I'd go to old record stores. I'd pay five cents for five old records. I'd get Al Jolson records, Eddie Cantor records, Ben Bernie, Rudy Vallee, Kate Smith.

I'd go on the radio. I'd say, "Ladies and gentlemen, this is a collector's item. It's worth five hundred dollars." I'd go back to the store the next day and buy some more records. I'd put down five pennies. The dealer would say, "Hey, come here, kid!" I said, "Whadaya mean '*kid*?'" He said, "I heard somebody on the radio last night saying those records are worth five hundred dollars!" So single handedly I more or less created the rare record market.

And then I got a call one day from Channel 7. They said, "Mr. Franklin?" I said, "Call me Joe." They said, "Joe, we'd like to talk to you about doing a show during the day." TV was only on the air then from five o'clock until sermonette. So they said, "If we give you an hour a day what kind of show would you do? We like the way you sound on the radio." So I said, "Well, what if I do a show with people more or less talking nose to nose, eyeball to eyeball?" They said, "No, you can't do that. The word is *television*. You've got to have vision, a seltzer battle, pratfalls, baggy pants burlesque skits." I said, "Well, if I can't do that, if I can't do a talk show, how about if I do a show with kids dancing to records?"

Rock 'n' roll was just getting started. They said, "Joe, you're out of your mind! "Who's gonna watch kids dancing to records?"

Who comes along but Dick Clark, who becomes a billionaire? So then I said, "How about I do a show of people singing the old-time songs?" They said, "Who's gonna watch that?" Mitch Miller comes along with *Sing along with Mitch!*

But I defied them. I did the first, pure organic, from-the-bones TV talk show. My first guest ever was Fannie Hurst, who wrote so many great books. And it has never stopped. I did forty-three years. I'm in *The Guinness Book of World Records*.

Mel   You answered my next question. *The Guinness Book of World Records*. That's amazing, Joe! Forty-three years. Do you have a ballpark figure, Joe, as to how many shows you did in all those years?

J.F.   Well, I think Richie Orenstein figured out twenty-eight thousand five hundred shows and half a million guests, five U.S. Presidents. I gave the first exposure ever on TV to Barbra Streisand, Bette Midler, Elvis Presley, Ann-Margaret, Woody Allen, Dustin Hoffman, Al Pacino, Liza Minnelli, Eddie Murphy, Garth Brooks.

Mel   It's a "who's who"—literally a "who's who" of show biz personalities!

J.F.   Everyone except Greta Garbo. Greta Garbo would watch me. We'd
         meet on the street, but she wouldn't come on my show. She wouldn't
         come on the air with anybody.

Mel   She wanted to be alone. Was that her classic line?

J.F.   Right!

Mel   Who impressed you? I mean, before many of these people became
         starts, of all the wonderful people you had, who did you, in your own
         mind, say, *This person is going to be a real heavyweight?*

J.F.   At the beginning? When they were unknown?

Mel   Yes.

J.F.   I would say Barbra Streisand. I would say Bette Midler, for sure. Let
         me think. Michael Jackson. I had Michael Jackson on five times with
         The Jackson Five. He was a cute little kid.

Mel   Was there anybody else besides Garbo that you wanted that did not do
         your show?

J.F.   The one I really wanted was Bing Crosby. And I finally got Bing. I got him
         through his wife. Bing, you know, in private life was romantically aloof.
         Bing was kind of cold. But that day with me he was warm and wonderful.

Mel   Well, I think that's due to you, Joe, because you always made your guests
         feel comfortable. Your show was like being in a living room with your
         friends and relatives. And it was great for me personally to do your show.

J.F.   Well, the one I was mostly concerned about was Bing, because I always
         thought of Bing as being sort of mechanically reproduced, but he was
         totally relaxed. I also ran across some people that I wanted on my
         show, but I was afraid to ask them. Only after they were dead did I find
         out they wanted to be invited.

         Some of the people that I was afraid to ask were Bert Lahr, Fred Allen,
         George S. Kaufman, Groucho Marx. I always found out later that they
         wanted to be invited. When Ruby Keeler was in *No, No, Nanette*, she was

the toast of the town. I wanted her on so badly, but I said to myself, *Everybody is chasing Ruby Keeler; I'm not going to bother her.* Later on I found out when the show closed she was waiting to be invited on my show.

Mel   Did you develop any sort of a personal relationship with any of the guests that you had over the years?

J.F.   Not really, I don't think so. I'm the only talk-show host who never had a talent coordinator, by the way. I had an audience every night they tell me of about fifteen million people. And I did all of my own booking.

Mel   You had basically an audience of fifteen million a show?

J.F.   Oh, yes. I was the first one on the cable.

Mel   That's right. Because I'm a Bostonian, and we got your Channel 9 show.

J.F.   That's right.

Mel   Are you doing anything in the way of performing or hosting any sort of show now?

J.F.   I'm on Bloomberg Radio. I do interviews. This week I've got Peter Falk, Mickey Rooney, Kitty Carlisle, Larry Hagman. I've got fantastic guests. Bloomberg Radio is heard all over the world.

Mel   Yes, we get Bloomberg Radio in Boston. I just hope you keep on going forever, Joe. You really are the best at what you do.

J.F.   Well, Mel, it means a lot to me. I've been a fan of yours for many, many centuries, many decades!

Mel   (Laughs)

J.F.   I love to reminisce with you.

Mel   Thank you, Joe. It's been a pleasure.

J.F.   Thank you, Mel.

Mickey Freeman

MICKEY FREEMAN (B. SHOLOM RUBINSTEIN) is an accomplished actor/comedian/writer. He is best remembered as Private Fielding Zimmerman on *The Phil Silvers Show*, which ran from 1955 to 1959. In that classic situation comedy, Private Fielding always seemed to be saying to the crafty Sergeant Bilko, "But Sarge …!" Freeman appeared on several other television programs (*Inner Sanctum*, *The Lloyd Bridges Show*, *Naked City*, *Lancer*), in motion pictures (including Shamus with Burt Reynolds) and on Broadway (*3 From Brooklyn*).

Mickey and I have a long-standing friendship. I think I've emceed him more than any other entertainer in the Catskill Mountains. He is a charming wit on and off the stage. Here is an interview I conducted with him on October 20, 2006…

Mel   Mickey Freeman, it's great to be with you. I've had the pleasure of emceeing you many times.

M.F.   Thank you, Mel.

Mel   You are a super comedian. Mickey, before we get into Bilko—and we'll talk a lot about Bilko—you are just a marvelous standup comedian.

M.F.   Thank you.

Mel   How did you get into comedy?

M.F.   I was the class wit in high school. I just sort of drifted into it. In the summer we had a bungalow colony in the Catskill Mountains. We were near the big hotels.

A fellow by the name of Dave Fisher was the social director of one of the hotels. I used to come in and sing "If You Knew Susie." I was so young that I wasn't casting a shadow!

So he said to me, "Would you like to work with me for next summer?" So he took me the next summer to a hotel called Sharon Springs, a very fancy hotel, a six-story-brick hotel.

Phil Silvers and Mickey Freeman as Sgt. Bilko and Pvt. Zimmerman

Mel   Where was that located?

M.F.   In Sharon Springs, New York.

Mel   In upstate New York?

M.F.   Yes, near Canada. People used to come there for the sulphur baths. So it was a good job, but it smelled bad! So from him I learned all the sketches. He taught me so very much.

And then I started doing comedy, and then I teamed up with George Sheck. We went to the Catskills, and he took care of the dancing and I took care of the comedy. Then I became a single and worked the Waldmere Hotel in Livingston Manor, and then I went to the White Row, which was the place. I followed Danny Kaye and Henny Youngman. That's how I broke into the business.

Mel   Before Bilko, did you do any acting in addition to standup?

M.F.   Yes. Leslie Neilsen is a friend of mine. I was on tour with his wife, who was a singer. When they got married I got them an apartment in my building. We were like brothers.

One night they invited me to a party. It was a Saturday night, and I play the ukulele.

Mel   I never knew that, Mick!

M.F.   Oh, yes. So I had a couple of drinks, and I played the ukulele and sang. This was a Saturday. Monday I got a call, "Mickey Freeman, my name is Everett Chambers. I'm the casting director for *Philco Playhouse.* I came into my office and there was a script calling for the world's fastest banjo player, and that's you." So I got the part.

Then I did a lot of dramatic shows. Then I worked with Imogene Coca. The casting director of CBS saw me on that show. He called me and I went down to read for the Bilko show.

Five days went by. I was in the bathroom, shaving. My wife Ann came running in. "There's a call from CBS They want to see you right away." I jumped into my car, and I started to drive, and fifteen minutes later I got a ticket. Not for speeding; for driving naked!

Mel   (Laughter)

M.F.   So I became Zimmerman on the *Bilko* show.

Mel   How many seasons?

M.F.   From 1957 to 1961.

Mel   And if memory serves me right, Mickey, you hit No. 1 in the ratings, didn't you?

M.F.   Well, we knocked off Berle. We were on opposite him on Tuesday night, and Berle used to come to see our filming. He said, "That's the funniest show I ever saw."

       It took us about three weeks to make it big. We did an appearance on *The Ed Sullivan Show* that made the people aware of our show.

Mel   The rest is history. Originally it had a different title, didn't it?

M.F.   *You'll Never Get Rich.*

Mel   How did they happen to switch from *You'll Never Get Rich* to *The Phil Silvers Show*?

M.F.   Well, Phil Silvers went to CBS and said, "I want to call it *The Phil Silvers Show*. The Vice President said, "You got it!"

Mel   So just like that it became *The Phil Silvers Show*. He was a comedy genius, wasn't he? What are your personal memories of Phil Silvers?

M.F.   He was a brilliant comedian. He was a compulsive gambler. He once lost $140,000 in a month in Las Vegas. Gambling was his big thing. The horses, card playing.

Mel   And unfortunately, that's probably what destroyed his marriage.

M.F.   Oh, yes. The gambling destroyed the marriage. His wife finally threw him out of the house.

Mel   She was a very pretty woman, if I remember. She was some sort of a beauty contest winner.

M.F.   She was on *The $64,000 Question*. She did the commercials.

Mel   Did any of his daughters go into the business?

M.F.   One of them did.

Mel   Mickey, they did a motion picture not too long ago on Sgt. Bilko. Did you see the movie?

M.F.   Ushers left the theatre! It was embarrassing. It was a shell. My God, a total waste of a film!

Mel   Well, I kind of figured that would happen even before I saw the movie. I mean, how do you replace a guy, with all due respect to Steve Martin, like Phil Silvers?

M.F.   No, no. They asked Red Buttons if he would be willing to take over the role the second season. And Red Buttons said, "That's Hara kari! There's nobody else to do this role. Phil Silvers was born [to play] Bilko.

Mel   Were they considering replacing Phil after the first season?

M.F.   Well, they had a little trouble with money, so they were just feeling around. But nobody could replace Phil.

Mel   Did you have a personal relationship with any of the other cast members?

M.F.   Yes, everybody.

Mel   Anybody particularly stick out in your mind?

M.F.   Oh, yes. Just yesterday I spoke to Alan Melvin. He was very funny on the show. He played Henshaw.

Mel   A great character actor.

M.F.   Harvey Lembeck, unfortunately, died of a heart attack.

Mel   He's gone many, many years; isn't he?

M.F.   Yes.

Mel   I assume it was the type of show where you really looked forward to going to work each and every week.

M.F.   Yes. My God. yes.

Mel   Where was the show filmed?

M.F.   Well, shows were filmed at the studio on 57th Street. It was the Dumont Studios.

Mel   In New York City?

M.F.   Yes. Live, in front of an audience.

Mel   Oh, it was live in front of an audience?

M.F.   Yes.

Mel   One last question: How did the residuals go in those days, and did you get residuals when the show went off?

M.F.   We got residuals. We got six residuals. Six times they paid us, and from then on, you could sell it in a butcher store for a pound of chuck! We got nothing after that. It plays in Europe. It plays all over the world.

        You know that I went to work on cruise ships all over the world. Wherever I went, people knew me. I came to Hong Kong. The manager of the Hong Kong Hilton said, "Zimmerman, it's you!" We stayed there for a week.

Mel   What was Zimmerman's first name?

M.F.   Fielding. Nat Hiken loved names!

Mel   Mickey, you've been great. Thank you so much.

M.F.   Mel, always a pleasure. Thank you. Love you. We go way back.

Mel   We sure do.

Mel Simons, Myron Cohen and Mickey Freeman

Larry Storch

Larry Storch

LAWRENCE SAMUEL "LARRY" STORCH (JANUARY 8, 1923) is an actor known for his comedic roles, especially that of the bumbling Corporal Randolph Agarn on, *F Troop*, a popular sitcom that ran from 1965 to 1967. Originally a standup comedian in his hometown of New York City, Storch fractured nightclub audiences with his many dialects, accents and impressions. (I had the pleasure of emceeing him many times and he was always sensational!) He was the host of *The Larry Storch Show* in the early 1950s and went on to guest star on countless situation comedies and variety shows. After finding success on television and in films, he returned to New York to focus on stage work. He is now semi-retired, but he still loves talking to fans—including *this* fan, as he did on January 15, 2008...

Mel   Good morning, Larry. It's Mel Simons.

L.S.   Oh, yes. Hello, Mel. Here we go. Now, how can I help you this morning?

Mel   I would like to do a little interview with you just for a few minutes.

L.S.   Okay. That sounds good. I just want to turn off my record player.

Mel   Sure.

L.S.   Be with you in one half minute.

Mel   Okay, Larry. Take your time.

L.S.   Okay. Back again. Here we go. Okay.

Mel   Okay, Larry. Well, of course—

L.S.   Now, wait. Where are you calling from?

Mel   I'm in Boston.

L.S.   Oh, boy!

Mel   Boston, I think you told me you got your start doing comedy in Boston.

L.S.   The Crawford House in Scollay Square.

Mel   Yeah, it's famous!

L.S.   In 1941, I remember, because I was working there when Pearl Harbor was bombed.

Mel   Oh, my!

L.S.   So I have that as a double memory for me, you know. And I've always loved Boston, I must say. Are you a Bostonian?

Mel   Oh, born and bred, absolutely.

L.S.   You know, when I first heard them talk like that, *Pahk the cah*, it absolutely knocked me out. You know, I thought it was the most wonderful dialect I'd ever heard.

Mel   Yes. We Bostonians do have an unusual way of talking. You know, Larry, everybody knows and loves you from *F Troop*, but I have had the pleasure of MCing you, and you're just a terrific comedian.

L.S.   Oh, gee, you're making my day, you know that, don't you?

Mel   Well, I tell it like it is, Larry. You are different—your impressions, your dialects. Did this all start when you were a younger?

L.S.   Oh, sure, yeah. I remember once when I first saw Claude Rains, and I must have been about seven years old. I saw him in *The Invisible Man*, and you know, I came home talking like Claude Rains, you know [Does a quick imitation].

Mel   (Laughter)

L.S.   It was one of those things. My mother said, "Oh, God!" But I could always be found when I wasn't in school, you know, as a kid in the balcony watching Edward G. Robinson and all those other guys, you know.

Mel   Yeah.

L.S.   And it started like that, you know, and I never did finish school actually.

Mel   How far did you go in school?

L.S.   I got into high school for twenty minutes, and the principal said to my mother, "He's better off getting that job that they've offered him rather than going four years in high school and coming out with, you know, nothing.

Mel   So you went right into comedy, into entertaining?

L. S.   Right. Yes.

Mel   And how did you begin? What was your start as far as entertaining professionally?

L.S.   Amateur hours…you would stand on the stage, all the people from the neighborhood in between the pictures. There were four pictures [movies]. It was like vaudeville almost, as I remembered, and you would do what you did best, sing or danced or whether it was play an instrument, and in my case I did [lapses into an impression of James Cagney]: "You dirty rat. I'm going to give it to you," and then at the end of the whole thing the MC would put his hand over your head or the fellow next to you or the lady next to you, and whoever received the most applause won the two dollars.

Mel   Two bucks! Wow!

L.S.   Oh and a lot of money that was in my day, boy.

Mel   I'll bet it was, Larry.

L.S.   That was 1933 and '4. You know, that time—

Mel   Golly. And how!

L.S.   And so that's the way I got my start, in amateur hours.

Mel   You know, I always heard a story that was credited to you, and I meant to ask you that last time I saw you, but when anybody does an imitation of Cary Grant and they go, "Judy, Judy, Judy," does that go back to you?

L.S.   Yeah. Even Cary Grant said, "You know who started that? An impressionist named Larry Storch." Well, you see when you say, "Judy," it was a good way to get his voice going where they would recognize him immediately, you know. "Judy, Judy, Judy." I mean, it was easy to do him after that.

Mel   Was there any truth to the rumor that it was Cary Grant talking to Judy Garland; is that how it started?

L.S.   I don't know. I don't remember who he was talking to, but I just started with that name, "Judy, Judy, Judy." So I remember meeting Cary Grant one time, and he said to me, "Hey, Larry Storch, wait up." He said, "I'm Cary Grant," and I said, "Oh, my God! I'll say you are!" I was so impressed, you know.

Mel   I'll bet. I hear he was a terrific gentleman.

L.S.   I just met him once or twice, but everybody knew him and loved him.

Mel   Now, you went into the Army.

L.S.   Navy.

Mel   Navy. I beg your pardon. Yes, it was the Navy, and I understand that you were in the Navy with Tony Curtis.

L.S,   We sailed from Vallejo, California, to Hawaii on the same submarine tender. It was *The Proteus,* and I'd been in the business, well, not a long time, and he was just thrilled. He said to me, "I'm going to be a movie star one day," as we're sailing toward Hawaii, "I'm going to be a big movie star one day," and I said, "Well, what about acting? Don't you have to…" Nah, nah. First things first."

          You know, get in line.

Mel   Wow!

L.S.   "First things first."

Mel   How did you find Tony Curtis as a person in those days?

L.S.   Oh, the nicest guy. We're friends to this day.

Mel   Oh, that's great.

L.S.   You know, we exchange telephone calls and Christmas cards and I love
         the boy. I mean, and do you know the funny thing, I said to him, "No,
         don't get into show business. It's too tough. It's tough"— *blah, blah,
         blah*—"No, no, no." And then after the war is over and he's struck it rich,
         he called me while I was in a Broadway show and said, "Come on out to
         Hollywood. We're doing a movie, and you're in a play at the same time."
         It was called, *Who Was That Lady?*

Mel   Oh, yes.

L.S.   Dean Martin was in it, and here Tony Curtis is giving me work.

Mel   Wow!

L.S.   You know, "Come on out. I've got another movie for you," and so our
         friendship really—as Tony Curtis used to say to me, "Two ships that
         passed in the night."

Mel   That's great.

L.S.   Well, one of the last ones that I did was with Tony on the road called
         Some Like It Hot.

Mel   Wow. Did you play any of the theatres in Boston?

L.S.   Did we play Boston? Yes, we did. We played The Wang—

Mel   Oh, The Wang. That's a big, enormous theatre, yes.

L.S.   I know, yes. We played The Wang Theatre.

Mel   When you got out of the Navy, what came next? I know you did a lot
         of Broadway shows. You did movies and, of course, nightclubs.

L.S.   Right.

Mel   But when you got out of the Navy what came next as far as your career?

L.S.   Magic. Let me tell you what happened. Here I am in my sailor suit,
the war is over. I'm released on the West Coast. I am hitch-hiking it
to New York. I want to see the country. I'm hitch-hiking in my sailor
suit. I stopped off a Palm Springs. I'm in a bar. The guy next to me is
Phil Harris. He says, "I see you got a musician's emblem." I was in the
band, so they made me a musician, and they put me in the band, so
that I could play. "Hey, we've got a funny cymbal player." I would
come down and do my act, you know.

Mel   Oh, very nice.

L.S.   Yeah. And anyway, I'm sitting next to Phil Harris. He says, "What did
you do before you were in?" I said, "I was a comic." "Get up on the
stage there in this bar and let me see what you can do."

Well, I did a couple of impersonations and Claude Rains and James– Well,
I didn't do James Mason at the time, but I did actors who were pretty well
known. He said, "Get in the car. We're going back to Hollywood."

He takes me to meet the Bing Crosby people, and the next thing I know
I'm on *The Frank Morgan Show*. I'm doing all the voices on *The Frank
Morgan Show* [Frank Morgan played the title role in *The Wizard of Oz*].

Mel   Sure.

L.S.-   And I was making about, oh—what were they paying me? Oh, and then,
this was the great thing! While I was doing those voices, Desi Arnaz—who
was married to Lucille Ball—he was opening at Ciro's and they needed an
act before Desi went on. They brought me down to Ciro's that afternoon
practically, that afternoon in my sailor suit. Oh, that's right. And Lucy
said, "Let me hear a couple of voices," and I did Frank Morgan. She said,
"All right. Wonderful." You go on before Desi. This is at Ciro's on
Hollywood Boulevard or Sunset it was. Sunset Boulevard. "You go on
before Desi. Do fifteen minutes, and then bring it along with 'Babaloo.'"

And that's the way it started from there. Isn't that magic?

Mel   It's unbelievable! It's like a fairy tale.

L.S.   And me fighting them all the way. I wanted to hitchhike back to New York in my sailor suit, and all of these things kept getting in my way.

Mel   And it all started [after] bumping into Phil Harris.

L.S.   Right. Sitting at a bar. I forget, what was the name of the bar? The Chi Chi or something like that. I can't remember the name of it. It was in Palm Springs.

Mel   You know, I'm an old Phil Harris fan, Larry. What was he like as a person?

L.S.   Oh, he was the greatest. You know, he adopted me in Las Vegas. I was at the Frontier—he was at the Frontier and I was at the Thunderbird, and opening night he sends me a telegram or he gives me a phone call. He says, "You gotta come on over here and save my life!" he said. "The president of Exxon Oil is in my dressing room, and he's telling me jokes, and he's as funny as an open grave."

Mel   (Laughter)

L.S.   "Come on over here and keep me company, boy." Well, anyway, I sat with him for two weeks in between shows. He takes off and he goes to Hollywood. He flew into Hollywood, and I had a telegram waiting from when he got off the plane, "Can't understand it. Why haven't you written?" And he sent me a telegram back that same day, "I've been sick." And he was a great storyteller, and he was a funny, really a legitimately funny guy. And a good drummer, by the way.

Mel   Oh, I didn't know that. I knew he was an orchestra leader at one time.

L.S.   Oh, he was a good drummer, yes.

Mel   I see. Pretty good-looking wife too, if you recall.

L.S.   Well, listen, Alice Faye was no slouch.

Mel   Yes, indeed. Now, I also want to ask you about replacing Jackie Gleason in the early 'fifties on *Cavalcade of Stars*. How did that come to be?

L.S.   I don't know how it came, but anyway he called me up to his office, and it was in The Sheraton Hotel, and he came out of his office in a bathrobe, and the office was marked "The Elephant Room." He weighed at that time about, oh, close to three hundred pounds or something like that.

Mel   Wow!

L.S.   And he said, "All right, Larry." He said, "I picked you to replace me. I'm going to be gone for thirteen weeks. I'm going to leave Art Carney with you, and you've got the show," he said. "Now, remember we're live. We're live." And he said, "Thousands of people watch." Millions was too much for everybody. We couldn't believe millions.

Mel   Yes.

L.S.   You know, but thousands was more in our backyard. "Thousands of people are going to be watching." So, are you ready, Mel?

Mel   Yup.

L.S.   He said, "Just don't use four-letter words."

Mel   (Laughter)

L.S.   He said, "Because we're on live. Can you remember that, Larry?"

Mel   (Continual laughter)

L.S.   And he said, "Good-bye and good luck." And that's the way—the only thing I can remember with the 1950 show, and I worked with Art Carney, whom I thought was the greatest. I was always in awe of Art Carney.

Mel   What was Art like off the tube as a person? What was he like?

L.S.   Well, we never really socialized. I loved him. We just never socialized. And do you know something? I didn't know that he blew some real good jazz piano.

Mel   Art Carney is a jazz pianist?

L.S   He was wonderful. If you watch some of the Jackie Gleason shows in color he sits down and plays some pretty good piano.

Mel   Wow! I was not aware of that.

L.S.   Oh, yeah.

Mel   I always loved him as a second banana to —

L.S.   To Gleason.

Mel   To Gleason.

L.S.   Oh, my God!

Mel   Kind of like a modern-day Laurel and Hardy.

L.S,   [Imitating Carney's character Art Norton]: "You're a beautiful kid, Ralphy boy."

Mel   Yes. (Laughter)

Now, I'm sure you did many of the variety shows like Ed Sullivan, for example. Tell us about that.

L.S.   I did three or four Ed Sullivan shows, and [imitating Sullivan]: "On our show let's really hear it out there," you know. But the funny thing is I was always scared silly, and they said he was a mean-spirited guy. He treated me well, but I had my respect for Ed Sullivan, and he gave a lot of people a chance to be seen, and he was very valuable to television.

Mel   [His show was on the air for] Twenty-three years.

L.S.   My God!

Mel   Amazing stat. Did you do any other TV shows before you started doing *F Troop*?

L.S.   Let me see. Not as many. *F Troop* was kind of the springboard for me.

Mel   Well, which leads me to my next question, Larry. How did you get that role?

L.S.   I think Forrest Tucker was mainly responsible as anybody else. I auditioned for the role of O'Rourke, and they said, "Very nice, but hold on. There's another guy here that will audition for Sgt. O'Rourke," and it was Forrest Tucker, and he said, "Well, listen, now. I'm going to need somebody to bounce jokes off of," and he said, "Think seriously about Larry getting the role." And that's how I got it, through Forrest Tucker. He was mainly the guy responsible for my getting in.

Mel   It was a great show.

L.S.   Oh, wasn't it something!

Mel   It was just a terrific show. I'm sure it's still on in reruns all over the world. You worked with Forrest Tucker. You worked with Ken Berry. What was it like to work with those two gentlemen?

L.S.   Oh, boy! The greatest. And then there was the other guy, Bob Steele, who was a great cowboy star.

Mel   Oh, yes. Of course.

L.S.   And then a guy named Jim Hampton. He played the bugler, and he was a very funny, kind [man]. And [Frank Dekova, the actor who played] the Indian Chief, Wild Eagle. He was Italian. He could rehearse his lines in Italian. It was very, very funny. And then there was Edward Everett Horton. [Imitating Horton]: "Oh, my word. Oh, dear."

Mel   Of course! (Laughter)

L.S.   [Continues the imitation]: "Oh, dear." [Laughs] I loved him.

Mel   You also had some interesting—

L.S.   I loved him.

Mel   Yeah, yeah, he was a terrific actor. I think Don Rickles did a show or two with you.

L.S.   He was Bald Eagle.

Mel   Bald Eagle, right. What was he like in those days?

L.S.   Oh, as noisy as ever and wonderful as ever, and, you know, we had some very important guests: Milton Berle, Phil Harris—Oh, let me see who.

Mel   Paul Lynde.

L.S.   Oh, boy.

Mel   Tell me about Paul Lynde. What was he like?

L.S.   Paul Lynde was wonderful. I mean, I had some scenes with him, and, you know, he was the same way as you remember him.

Mel   That's great.

L. S.   Oh, I was crazy about him.

Mel   How about Uncle Miltie? What was he like to work with?

L.S.   Oh, Milton Berle, I have some memories about Milton Berle. I was in a small nightclub in New York one time. He came in to see the show, and he said to me—he called me over to the table. He said, "Listen, you've got some talent, but you gotta have some jokes," and he wrote out about ten jokes for me to tell. He changed my whole act around in some little sleazy nightclub in New York, and that's when I enlisted into the Navy. It would have been 1941, and so Milton Berle rewrote my whole act for me in between shows.

Mel   He was a very, very generous person, wasn't he?

L.S.   Oh, yes. I mean, if he likes you, yes he was. And we got along well. He played Wise Owl on the—

Mel   Oh, yes.

L.S.   Very funny guy.

Mel   Who created *F Troop*, and who wrote it?

L.S.   Who created it? I can't—I wish I knew.

Mel   How about the writers?

L.S.   There were a lot of writers, but there was one guy named Arthur Julien, J-U-L-I-E-N. He had a touch of Nat Hiken in him and Larry Gelbart in him.

Mel   Wow!

L.S.   He had all that talent in him, but the Nat Hiken and the Gelbart touch in him, and he was the guy that I liked most. And there were some very good writers. I just can't remember their names, but Arthur Julien was a writer that I adored, and indeed, all the actors and actresses on that—

Mel   Well, the blend of both the writers and the actors was absolutely terrific. Just one of the greatest sitcoms ever!

L.S.   It was really something, really.

Mel   Now, when *F Troop* went off the air, then you went back to doing clubs and concerts and things of that nature?

L.S.   I went back on the Broadway stage.

Mel   Now, tell us about some of the shows you did on Broadway.

L.S.   Oh, I was in—the last one I did was *Sly Fox* at The Ethel Barrymore Theatre.

Mel   Famous, sure.

L.S.   And then I've been with Reba McIntyre in *Annie Get Your Gun.*

Mel   Oh, wow!

L.S.   And let me see, I was in *Porgy and Bess* in Lincoln Center, and with some of the great opera stars.

Mel   You also did many movies throughout your career, Larry.

L.S.   Yes.

Mel   Any particular favorites?

L.S.   Let me see. Well, the ones I did with Tony Curtis were always my favorites, I think. He always had some nutty casts. I mean, Dean Martin in one, and Phil Silvers in *40 Pounds of Trouble,* and it was always comedy with Tony.

Indeed, that's what I've done most of the time, but anyway, now I'm on the Broadway stage. I really got a lot of chances to—I played a Russian spy. I was Sakini in *The House of August Moon*, and so I was able to do dialects.

Mel   Yeah. I think that's your first love; isn't it, when it comes to doing stand-up?

L.S.   Oh, dialects, yeah.

Mel   I mean, nobody does dialects like you.

L.S.   And I love to do them. You know, if you can tell a joke—I always tell guys who want to be comics, "If you can tell a joke," which is obsolete anymore. Nobody tells stories that last two or three minutes. But if you could do them in dialect, you were halfway home.

Mel   Then the next big TV show, you've got some longevity out of this, was the Saturday morning TV show, *Ghost Busters*.

L.S.   Oh, you remember that.

Mel   I certainly do. What are your memories of that show?

L.S.   The gorilla had the brain of the trio. He did the driving, the cooking, the thinking so far as Tucker and I, and we used to say, "Only God can make a trio!"

Mel   (Laughter)

L.S.   And that was us.

Mel   Well, it was a fun show.

L.S.   Oh, yeah.

Mel   What a great career you have had, Larry, going back to your start in Boston. Are you doing anything today as far as entertaining?

L.S.   No. No. And I don't—that's the way I like it now.

Mel   So basically you're retired?

L.S.   Yes.

Mel   You know, comedy has changed so much. The profanity amazes me.

L.S.   Oh, come on.

Mel   To go into a comedy club nowadays, and a comedian comes out and it's just a barrage of four-letter words.

L.S.   I know, I know.

Mel   I've always said that comedy today has gone the route of music, because I think today's music is the worst. Do any of the newer comics make you laugh? Is there anybody you particularly—

L.S.   I can't think of anybody I would leave the house to go see in person.

Mel   I feel the same way.

L.S.   I can't think of anybody.

Mel   Yeah. There's really nobody around to replace people like you, Milton Berle, Henny Youngman, Morey [Amsterdam]. It's totally a different ballgame today.

L.S.   It is, right. I mean, there were nightclubs all over the city. There was a hundred nightclubs, and vaudeville. Everywhere you turned there was vaudeville—I mean, I played the Paramount with Perry Como and Nat Cole, and to be on a bill with those guys, my God! I was like a kid. I wanted to ask them for their autographs.

Mel   You really have worked with the "who's who" of entertainers over the years.

L.S.   Oh, indeed I have, and I'm very proud of that.

Mel   Absolutely. Let me ask you this: If you had to pick perhaps your two or three favorite entertainers as people—not as entertainers but as people—who did you work with that you enjoyed?

L.S.   Oh, Sarah Vaughan.

Mel   As a person?

L.S.   Oh, yeah. I mean, she was wonderful to me. Sarah Vaughan. Let me— oh my God, there are just so many of them, who were so nice. Billy DeWolf, he was my idol. Do you remember Billy DeWolf?

Mel   I certainly do. Another great dialectician.

L.S.   And I think he came out of Boston.

Mel   Yes, he was. He was a Bostonian, I believe.

L.S.   A Bostonian, yes. We were in the Navy together.

Mel   Oh, no kidding.

L.S.   But I was his admirer long before we got into the Navy, and then I was lucky to work with him half of the war in a short-lived series called *The Queen and I.*

Mel   No, I don't recall that, Larry.

L.S.   No—don't even try. Don't even try.

Mel   (Laughter) Didn't quite make it, huh?

L.S.   Right.

Mel   Well, you know, it's been such a thrill to talk to you. I MC'd you I'm going to guess around 1980 or '81 at The Brickman Hotel in the Catskills. I don't know if you remember Brickman's

L.S.   Sure.

Mel   But you tore the place apart. You were just great.

L.S.   Oh, thank you.

Mel   People spoke about you for days after your performance.

L.S.   Well, that's gotta stop!

Mel   And I found it just a great experience to MC you where I had been a fan of yours for so many years, I mean, I'm a fan of yours, you know, before *F Troop*.

L.S.   Well, I appreciate that, really.

Mel   Well, Larry, I want to thank you so much. You have been just wonderful, as I knew you would be, and I speak as a great admirer of yours for many, many years. I thank you for a terrific interview.

L.S.   Okay. My pleasure, Mel.

Mel   And I hope to see you real soon.

L.S.   Okay. Take care.

About the Author

MEL SIMONS has amassed one of the world's largest old-time radio and television show collections. His knowledge of vintage entertainment is on display in his acclaimed books and lectures on the subject. Mel lives in Boston and can be heard on WBZ Radio.

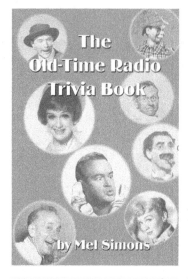
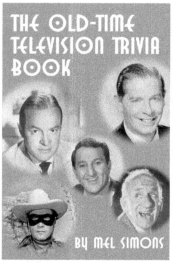

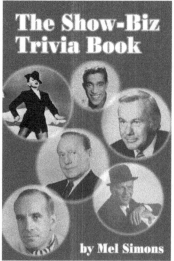

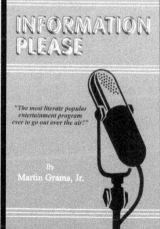

Printed in the USA
CPSIA information can be obtained
at www.ICGtesting.com
JSHW060929171124
73588JS00013B/262